Tax Guide 203

THE PROS & CONS OF LLCs

by

Holmes F. Crouch
Tax Specialist

Published by

Allyear Tax Guides
20484 Glen Brae Drive
Saratoga, CA 95070

ISBN-13: 9780944817803
ISBN-10: 0944817807

LCCN 2006930826

Printed in U.S.A.

Series 200
Investors & Businesses

Tax Guide 203

THE PROS & CONS OF LLCs

For other titles in print, see page 224.

The author: **Holmes F. Crouch**
For more about the author, see page 221.

PREFACE

If you are a knowledge-seeking **taxpayer** looking for information, this book can be helpful to you. It is designed to be read — from cover to cover — in about eight hours. Or, it can be "skim-read" in about 30 minutes.

Either way, you are treated to **tax knowledge** . . . *beyond the ordinary*. The "beyond" is that which cannot be found in IRS publications, the IRS web site, IRS e-file instructions, or tax software programs.

Taxpayers have different levels of interest in a selected subject. For this reason, this book starts with introductory fundamentals and progresses onward. You can verify the progression by chapter and section in the table of contents. In the text, "applicable law" is quoted in pertinent part. Key phrases and key tax forms are emphasized. Real-life examples are given . . . in down-to-earth style.

This book has 12 chapters. This number provides depth without cross-subject rambling. Each chapter starts with a head summary of meaningful information.

To aid in your skim-reading, informative diagrams and tables are placed strategically throughout the text. By leafing through page by page, reading the summaries and section headings, and glancing at the diagrams and tables, you can get a good handle on the matters covered.

Effort has been made to update and incorporate all of the latest tax law changes that are *significant* to the title subject. However, "beyond the ordinary" does not encompass every conceivable variant of fact and law that might give rise to protracted dispute and litigation. Consequently, if a particular statement or paragraph is crucial to your own specific case, you are urged to seek professional counseling. Otherwise, the information presented is general and is designed for a broad range of reader interests.

The Author

INTRODUCTION

The fear in the heart of every owner of an unincorporated business is the potential of a lawsuit. In such a litigious society as the United States, it is not a question of "if" a lawsuit will occur. It is only a matter of time "when" it will occur. When it does, it will be based on some perceived wrongdoing by the business entity itself, or on some alleged misconduct by an owner, manager, employee, or agent thereof. Regardless of what the business activity may be, there is always **that threat** out there.

The target for attack is not so much the assets of the business itself. Most small and closely-held businesses barely keep enough capital on hand to meet their operating needs. And rarely are they isolated with asset/liability balance sheets. Because so, the primary target for lawsuit is the personal assets of the principals of the business: their homes, bank accounts, investments, realty holdings, and future earnings. These targets are all fair game under the "alter ego" theory for piercing the entity shield.

There is an inherent injustice in piercing the entity shield of a small business with extraneous lawsuits having no direct connection to the conduct or misconduct of its owners and managers. For well over 30 years, various state legislatures have wrestled with this problem. To one degree or another, remedial effort was directed at *limiting* the personal liability of unincorporated entrepreneurs, without giving them a green light to violate ordinary business and contract law. Finally, in early 1997, all 50 states (plus the District of Columbia) have agreed upon a new entity form: the LIMITED LIABILITY COMPANY (**LLC**).

So new is the operational concept of an LLC that the Internal Revenue Code does not use the term in any of its business-related sections and subsections. Instead, it is embodied in the term "eligible entity" in Regulation § 301.7701-3: *Classification of certain business entities*. Its two opening sentences read—

> *A business entity that is not classified as a corporation . . . (an eligible entity) can elect its classification for federal tax purposes. An eligible entity with at least two members can elect to be classified as . . . [an LLC] partnership.*

In other words, under federal tax law, an LLC is a *partnership* if it has two or more members. If there is only one member, the LLC is either a proprietorship or a corporation. If a sole owner elects to be a corporation, there is no point in being an LLC. Hence, for federal purposes, there are two types of LLCs: a proprietorship LLC and a partnership LLC. The situation is different under each state law where the LLC is formed.

In the meantime, we have this book: ***The Pros & Cons of LLCs***. Our objective is to sidestep the promotional hype and excitement associated with LLCs, and take a closer look at the serious side of this "new darling" of unincorporated business. First and foremost, an LLC is a profit-seeking business. It is not a tax shelter, nor is it some scam operation. When profits are made, there are taxes to pay. But the manner of doing so involves some unique characteristics of an LLC's own. This is because an LLC is a hybridized entity with the managerial flexibility of a proprietorship, the profit and loss pass-through benefits of a partnership, and the limited personal liability trump card of a full-fledged C corporation.

The feature of "limited liability" does not bestow upon an LLC a free-wheeling, responsibility-avoiding arrangement for exploitative entrepreneurship. Yes, there is intrigue and excitement in those two letters "LL". But they do not extend a right of passage to lots of money without incurring personal obligation in some manner. This is particularly true for con artists who are attracted to multi-member LLCs the way they've been attracted to limited partnerships in years past.

The painful reality is that there are articles of organization to be filed with state authorities and fees to be paid; there are operating agreements to be worked out; there is a minimum capital base to be maintained; there are at-risk and loss limitation rules to be heeded; there are books and records to be kept; there are balance sheets to be balanced; there are tax returns to be filed; and there are contracts with customers, creditors, and suppliers to be honored. In the end, every LLC has to take its place in line demonstrating responsible behavior, as do other entities, both corporate and noncorporate.

CONTENTS

Chapter	Page

1

A HYBRIDIZED ENTITY

An LLC Is Not A Corporation, Though It Has The Personal Liability Protection Of Both C And S Corporations. An LLC Is More Like A Partnership Where Each Member Has Both The Ownership And Management Rights Of A Proprietorship. Statutorily, There Is No Limit To The Number And Type Of Members Permitted. At Some Number, Though, Prudence And Reality Close In To Force Compliance With The SHARING AGREEMENT That All Members Have Signed. As With any Traditional Business, An LLC Must Actively Seek A Profit. After Which, All Earnings And Losses Are "Passed Through" Prorata To Individual Members.

As of January 1997, all 50 states plus the District of Columbia had legislated a new type of business entity called: Limited Liability Company (LLC). Yet, to this date, there is no separate tax recognition of an LLC in the Internal Revenue Code (IRC). In other words, Congress has enacted no revenue laws expressly addressing LLCs as it has done for proprietorships, partnerships, S corporations, and C corporations. So, how do present-day LLCs fit into IRS's procedures for tax reportings and tax law compliances?

Answer: An LLC is a "wedged-in" entity. It is so via an IRS-prepared sub-regulation under IRC Section 7701: *Definitions*. Subsection (a) thereof lists 48 definitional terms, the first three of which are: (1) person, (2) partnership, and (3) corporation. Of the 45 remaining definitional items, the term LLC — or its equivalent: *eligible entity* — does not appear. Other subsections (b) through

(o) [14 in all] explain other tax related definitions but, again, no mention of an LLC is made. Now what?

The nearest tax law on point (Congressionally enacted) is subsection 7701(l): *Regulations Relating to Conduit Arrangements*. A conduit (or pass-through) arrangement is—

> *Any multi-party financing transaction . . . where the* [IRS] *determines that* **recharacterization** *is appropriate to prevent avoidance of any tax imposed by this title* [the Internal Revenue Code]. [Emphasis added.]

From this statutory authority, the IRS has adopted Regulation § 301.7701-3T(h)(3): *Classification of Certain Business Entities: Limited Liability Companies*. We are going to expound on this regulation in Chapter 4: IRS Election Form 8852.

Meanwhile, we want to describe the general features of an LLC as it relates to the existing features of a proprietorship, partnership, S corporation, and C corporation. Because no specific tax code section on LLCs exists, we want to describe how an LLC is basically a hybrid of these four traditional business forms. For a quick overview of this hybridizing — or "wedging-in" — principle, we present Figure 1.1. As a wedge-in entity, there is no need for any Congressional tax statute expressly addressing LLCs.

The "Tax Imposition" Laws

Recall from the partial citation of Section 7701 (l) above, the reference to "any tax imposed" by the IR Code. If you quick-glance at the Table of Contents of the IR Code, you'll find that there are only two predominantly tax imposition sections. There is Section 1: *Tax Imposed (on Individuals)* and Section 11: *Tax Imposed (on Corporations)*. Yes, there are other taxes imposed, but these two predominate with respect to the taxation of income generated. Search as long as you want, but you'll not find any tax impositions expressly on partnerships, LLCs, or S corporations. What is the explanation?

Answer: There is an inference drawn from subsection 1(h)(10): *Pass-Through Entity Defined*. Included in this definition are a partnership, an S corporation, and *a qualified electing fund.* We interpret this last entity to include an LLC which is an "eligible entity" under IRS Regulation § 301.7701-3T(h)(3) above. Thus, at this point we have informed you that an LLC is a qualified pass-through entity. Indeed it is; it definitely is not taxed as a C corporation.

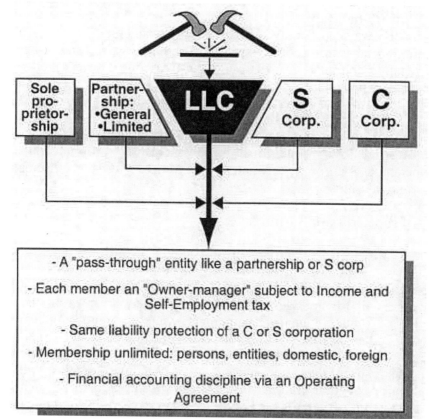

Fig. 1.1 - The "Hybridization" of an LLC From Traditional Businesses

As a pass-through entity, an LLC — like a partnership and S corporation — is taxed at each individual owner's filing status rate. There are four such rates, namely:

Sec. 1(a) — Married individuals filing jointly
Sec. 1(b) — Heads of households
Sec. 1(c) — Unmarried (single) individuals

Sec. 1(d) — Married individuals filing separately

As you can sense on your own, many different individuals can participate in an LLC arrangement. This feature, plus the fact that an LLC is not entity taxed, is the birth seed for abusive transactions involving LLCs. We'll comment on possible abuses in Chapter 9: Con Artistry Indicators.

By the way, an "entity" is a business arrangement whereby its accounting aspects (income, deductions, credits, gains, and losses) are separate and apart from those of the individual owners thereof. Keeping such accounting true and accurate at all times is one of the key ingredients for preserving the limited liability protection of an LLC. More on this in Chapter 3: Liability of Members.

In the meantime, let us explore the hybridized features of an LLC with respect to the traditional business forms: proprietorships, partnerships, S corporations, and C corporations. First, we'll touch on proprietorships.

LLC Proprietorship Features

A proprietorship is a one-person beehive of business activity. One person owns the business 100%. He contributes all necessary capital, property, and services to keep the business afloat and solvent at all times. He is the owner-manager; he does all the buying of (and paying for) equipment, materials, and supplies; employs others as employees, contractors, and consultants. He can use any fictitious business name that he wants so long as no one else has chosen the same name. As a safeguard against the duplication of dba (*doing business as*) business names, each proprietorship owner files a *Fictitious Business Name Statement* with the Clerk's office of the county within which the business operates. Depending on the particular state in question, the statement is filed every five years or so. There is no simpler way to start up and run a business than in sole proprietorship form. No associates are involved; one does his own thing.

The weakness of a sole proprietorship is that the personal assets of the owner, outside of the business operation, are fully exposed to mischievous lawsuits. Business liability insurance can be purchased, but such insurance can become very expensive (particularly for construction, transportation, manufacturing, and high-profile professional activities).

A sole proprietor files a business tax return known as Schedule C (Form 1040): *Profit or Loss from Business* and/or Schedule F (Form 1040): *Profit or Loss from Farming*. If there is a net profit from Schedule C or Schedule F, in addition to ordinary income tax there is a second tax to pay. It is called: *Self-Employment Tax* (Schedule SE). This is not a second income tax; it is a social security and medicare tax similar to that imposed on managers and employees of other entity businesses. Nevertheless, it is a second tax to pay on an individual's personal service income. For free-wheeling LLC entrepreneurs, the self-employment tax is an anathema — something to be avoided at all costs. Avoiding the SE tax is virtually impossible where the type of LLC business requires the personal services of the owners thereof.

Altogether, there are three features of a proprietorship that hybridize into the features of an LLC. These are:

(1) Ordinary income taxed at individual rates,
(2) The self-employment tax on personal services performed for the LLC; and
(3) The owner-manager prerogatives of a privately owned enterprise.

A proprietorship files **Form 1040:** *U.S. Individual Income Tax Return* . . . every calendar year.

LLC C-Corporation Features

At the other end of the spectrum where corporate tax rates apply is the C-type corporation. A C corporation is the premier among all business forms. Absent fraud and malfeasance by the directors and managers thereof, the *corporate shield* fully protects the shareholders and operating personnel from personal liability for corporate bungling of its business affairs. Good corporate tax and financial accounting is the bulwark of limited liability protection. See our Figure 1.2 in this regard.

The admirable features of a C corporation that hybridize into an LLC are its:

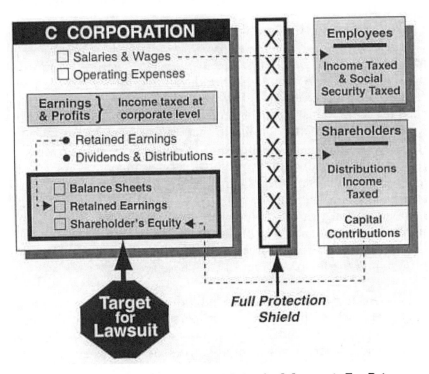

Fig. 1.2 - The "Accounting Isolation" Role of a C Corporate Tax Return

(1)   continuity of life (indefinite when legally franchised under state law);

(2)   centralization of management (from within with external oversight);

(3)   free association of participants (unlimited in number) to engage in any lawful business and divide its profits; and

(4)   liability for corporate debts is directed strictly at all available corporate property.

Editorial Note: Ownership in a C corporation can consist of: (i) active individuals, (ii) passive individuals, (iii) corporations (C or S), (iv) partnerships (general or limited); (v) exempt organizations, (vi) estates and trusts, (vii) nominees, and (viii) LLCs. Domestic and foreign shareholders can participate. When registered as "securities," shares can be sold publicly, after which no shareholder can be held personally liable.

A C corporation files **Form 1120**: *U.S. Corporation Income Tax Return* . . . every fiscal year.

There are two weaknesses of C corporations from the perspective of an LLC. One, there is no direct pass-through of the corporate income gains, losses, deductions, and credits to its owners. Yes, dividends are distributed but only after corporate taxes have been paid. So dividends are taxed a second time. The second weakness is that there are numerous participants, corporate securities (stocks, bonds, debt instruments), and registrations and regulations imposed at both the state and federal levels. As a consequence, a C corporation involves greater formality and rigidity than is tolerable by free-spirited entrepreneurs.

LLC S-Corporation Features

An S corporation is an incorporated entity under state law. As such, specific Rules and Bylaws must be established to set the tone of its financial discipline and to record separately the contributions and withdrawals of its shareholders. With this financial accounting isolation, an S corporation provides the same limited liability protection of a C corporation (depicted in Figure 1.2). This point is worthy of note by LLC aspirants.

There is one clear advantage of an S corporation over a C type. There is no double income taxation. All profits, losses, and credits are passed directly through to the individual shareholders in proportion to their shareholding interests. Each shareholder pays income tax on the distributive share of the S corporation that he/she receives. That is, the S corporation itself generally pays no income tax . . . at the federal level. This, too, is a point worthy of note by LLC aspirants.

For this pass-through tax benefit, certain shareholder restrictions apply. First off, the number of shareholders is limited to 100. Secondly, all shareholders must be individual persons who are either U.S. citizens or U.S. residents. And, thirdly, only one class of stock can be issued (which must have voting rights). The stock is required to be registered at the state level, but is limited to private sales only. No public offering of S stock is authorized. For these reasons and others, an S corporation is also referred to as a small business corporation (the "S" for "small").

An S corporation files **Form 1120S:** *U.S. Income Tax Return for an S corporation.* The "income tax" aspect is limited to built-in capital gains from C corporation conversions, and to the excess passive income (over 25%) derived from interest, dividends, rents, and royalties. Otherwise, nonpassive income is not taxed.

At the federal level, an S corporation is an *elective entity.* That is, to be allowed the pass-through benefits, an IRS Form 2553: **Election by Small Business Corporations** has to be executed. This election must be made within $2^{1/2}$ months of its date of state law incorporation. To be valid, the **unanimous consent** of all shareholders must be obtained. This can be a Herculean task when 25, 50, 75, or 100 shareholders are involved.

With too many owner-bosses, controversies can erupt because of differences in tax interests. A high income shareholder may not want any S corporation profits passed through to him, though he probably would want the losses, deductions, and credits to pass through. Conversely, a low income shareholder would certainly want the income, profits, and gains passed through, but not the losses. An S corporation's pass-throughs are directly proportional to each participant's number of days, dollars, and shares involved. Similar elective consent is a fundamental feature of an LLC.

Overall, the features of an S corporation that hybridize into a profit-oriented business LLC are:

(1) The pass-through of all earnings and profits to individual shareholders with no entity tax whatsoever.

(2) The relative informality and flexibility of the corporate structure, while still retaining the liability shield protection of a C corporation.

(3) The registration process in the state of business origin; the process alone confers an officially recognized "legal entity" status.

Even so, there are certain disadvantages of an S corporation for LLC purposes. All shareholders must be domestic individuals: neither foreigners nor entities are allowed. All distributive sharing is based on each shareholder's percentage of ownership: no flexibility in sharing is allowed. Whatever the disadvantages may be, they are easily circumvented by a partnership arrangement.

General Partnership Features

In its most rudimentary form, a partnership is the voluntary association of two or more persons to conduct their active business affairs in joint venture form. There can be *any* two or more participants: two or more individuals, two or more entities, any combination of individuals and entities, and any residency status, domestic or foreign. Without other qualifications, an associative arrangement of this type is called: *a general partnership.*

Unlike an S corporation, a partnership issues no shares of stock. It issues partnership interests. The term "interest" is an *ownership interest* fractionalized as a percentage of the total book value of the enterprise. Theoretically, there is no upper limit to the number of participants that can be partners of a partnership. But when the number reaches 100 or more, the partnership interests become fractioned and subfractioned to the point where the subfractional interests begin to take on the investor role of shares in a corporation. When this happens, the IRS can disregard the partnership arrangement and require that the association of interest holders be taxed as a C corporation. The partnership can, however, elect to be treated as a *Publicly Traded Partnership* (PTP) whose interests can be publicly traded on established primary and secondary securities markets. No LLC aspirant would tolerate the regulatory oversight of a PTP.

In federal tax parlance, a bona fide partnership is a *Subchapter K* entity. The "K" refers to that batch of 36 separate and specific sections in the Internal Revenue Code titled: **Partners and Partnerships.** The first of these 36 sections is Section 701: **Partners, Not Partnerships, Subject to Tax.** This key lead-off section reads in full—

> *A partnership as such shall not be subject to income tax. Persons carrying on business as partners shall be liable for income tax only in their separate capacities.*

In other words, a partnership acts as a conduit through which tax consequences flow to each partner separately (whether individual or entity). A portion of the partnership income, equal to the partner's distributive share, is then reported and taxed on each partner's separate tax return. The partners are liable for tax on all partnership income regardless of whether the income is distributed or retained as capital. This is the precursor to the flow-through concept for all distributive sharing entities: limited partnerships, LLCs, S corporations, estates, and trusts.

The mechanics of flow-through (pass-through) are done on a **Schedule K-1** (Form 1065): *Partner's Share of Income, Deductions, Credits, etc.* [*Ed. Note*: To remind you again, the letter "K" derives from reference to subchapter K of the IR Code.] The partnership Form 1065 is titled: *U.S. Return of Partnership Income*. The Schedule K-1 is prepared in accordance with the Partnership Agreement which, among other items, spells out the distributive sharing arrangement among the partners. The agreed-to arrangement can enable a high-income partner to receive a greater portion of the losses, credits, and deductions, in deference to low-income partners who prefer a greater portion of partnership income and gains. This one feature alone makes partnerships much more attractive to LLC aspirants than an S corporation where the "sharing" is share-percentage fixed.

The general concept immediately above is portrayed in Figure 1.3. The Partnership Agreement, which we label functionally in Figure 1.3 as a "Sharing Agreement," must prescribe all enforceable terms of entity operations. This includes the relative amounts of profit sharing, loss sharing, debt sharing, liability sharing, and capital sharing among all partners.

Limited Partnership Features

From a participant's personal liability perspective, there are two major disadvantages to a general partnership. Foremost is that there are too many bosses. Every general partner is an owner-manager with an equal say in how the joint enterprise is run. For two or three member partnerships, equal-say bosses can work quite well. Even up to five members can work satisfactorily, provided each is specifically assigned his or her operational duties. Beyond five member partnerships, internal conflicts and bickerings develop, and reciprocal accusations of wrongdoings flare. Soon, the point is reached where the sharing arrangement totally breaks down. Then ugly lawsuits fly back and forth.

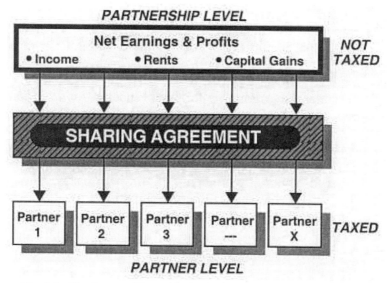

Fig. 1.3 - The Income "Pass-Through" Concept of a Partnership

The second major disadvantage is that there is no liability protection of the conscientious partner against the misdeeds of other, more cavalier partners. Under general partnership principles, all partners are co-liable — called: *joint and several liability* — for all misdeeds within the partnership as well as those **by** the partnership. The personal assets of each partner beyond his/her partnership interests are in jeopardy.

To overcome these two truly major deterrents, many states have enacted a *Limited Partnership* law. In a limited partnership, at least one member must be a general partner and one or more members may be limited partners. The general partner (or partners — rarely more than three) each itself is either a C or S corporation. This incorporation status of the general partner gives each the liability shield protection it needs. With such protection, the general partner(s) can manage the business more effectively.

The limited partners, usually far more than a few, have no management role whatsoever. Thus, they can create no misdeeds within the partnership itself. They are treated as passive investors, with all of the flow-through benefits of a general partnership. If a partnership misdeed occurs, the limited partners risk only their investment in the partnership. Their personal assets outside of the partnership are fully shielded.

A limited partnership (LP) files the same federal tax return as does a general partnership (GP). There's a checkbox difference only. We'll explain shortly below.

Some states have gone so far as to enact a *Limited Liability Partnership* law (LLP). The sponsors of LLP state legislation are usually high-income professional persons: doctors, lawyers, accountants, actuaries, etc. Even so, an LLP files the same federal tax return as does a GP. Again, there is a checkbox difference.

Whether a general partnership, a limited partnership, or a limited liability partnership, all partnerships file **Form 1065**: *U.S. Return of Partnership Income*.

Degrees of Work Participation

There is one particular aspect of an LLC that is not addressed in the commentary above. This omission has to do with the degree of participation directly in the business by the LLC members themselves. All members are essentially proprietors. That is, each owns a slice of the business and, as such, is expected to contribute sufficient personal services to generate nutrients (income, profit, gain) to keep that slice alive. In other words, it is more helpful to think of an LLC as a "hands on" operation than would be the case for partnerships and corporations.

The term "participation" is defined in the instructions to proprietorship Schedules C and F (Form 1040) as—

Participation . . . generally includes any work you did in connection with an activity **if you owned an interest in the activity at the time you did the work.** *The capacity in which you did the work does not matter.* [It only matters that] *the work you do is that which an owner would customarily do to protect his interests in the same type of activity* [as yours].

The work performed in an activity must be genuine, and must relate to its ongoing needs. Make-work won't do. The degree of participation distinguishes the types of activities than an LLC may engage in.

The IRS has identified three degrees of work participation and the activities to which they relate. These are—

1. Material participation
   — regular, continuous, daily, for ongoing supervision of operations
   — most applicable to the **core** activity of an enterprise.

2. Active participation
   — regularly on-call, as needed, for the use and maintenance of property
   — most applicable to rental activities such as real estate, vehicles, and equipment.

3. Passive participation
   — making decisions when to buy and when to sell investment assets
   — most applicable to portfolio-type activities, such as stocks, bonds, mutual funds, collectibles, etc. where the "holding period" is the agent for income, capital gain, or capital loss.

What do these three degrees of work participation by LLC owners tell us?

Answer: They define the heart of uniqueness of an LLC. That is, an LLC is responsibly capable of conducting simultaneously three different types of income-producing activities. Having productive hands-on activities means greater chance of entrepreneurial success, and less chance for gimmickry and scams.

Which LLC Tax Form?

We tell you right now that there is no federal tax form expressly for an LLC. For example, there is no such form as *Form 1068: U.S. Return of LLC Income.* Does this mean that an LLC is exempt from liability for federal tax? After all, don't the letters "LL" stand for **Limited Liability**? Wouldn't this include limited liability against federal tax? We are pulling your leg, of course. We know that you know better.

If you'll glance back at our discoursings above, you will note that we have identified four different federal tax forms. Those mentioned are:

- Proprietorship — **Form 1040**: U.S. Individual Income Tax Return

- C Corporation — **Form 1120**: U.S. Corporation Income Tax Return

- S Corporation — **Form 1120S**: U.S. Income Tax Return for an S Corporation

- Partnership — **Form 1065**: U.S. Return of Partnership Income

We now must tell you that an LLC files federal **Form 1065**: *U.S. Return of Partnership Income*. Then on page 2 thereof, you check one of the six boxes as applicable, namely:

a. Domestic general partnership .... ☐

b. Domestic limited partnership .... ☐

c. Domestic limited liability company .... ☒

d. Domestic limited liability partnership ...... ☐

e. Foreign partnership .... ☐

f. Other ▶_____ .... ☐

After checking box c, you follow all of the federal tax accounting rules that apply to partnerships. These rules can be both challenging and puzzling. Do be patient, as we'll methodically describe them in subsequent chapters.

2

STATE LAW FORMATION

There Are Four Steps In The Formation Of An LLC. First, There Is Need To Select A Name And "Reserve It" With The Secretary Of State In Which You Intend To Do Business. Next, There Is Need For An Organizational Meeting To Designate Who Among The Participants Shall Be The "Organizer" For Filing ARTICLES OF ORGANIZATION. Third, There Is A "Statement Of Information" Designating The Principal Office Where Records Will Be Kept, Names Of Managers And Members, And Agent For Service Of Legal Process. Fourth Is An OPERATING AGREEMENT Which Only LLC Members Have The Power To Adopt, Alter, Or Amend.

The formation of a Limited Liability Company (LLC) comes under state law: not under federal law. As of April 1, 1997, all 50 states and the District of Columbia have enacted LLC statutes. The statutes vary to some degree, depending on each state's own legal practices for dealing with business activities and citizen complaints that arise from them. For this reason, it is wise to think always that the legal aspects of an LLC are a state jurisdictional matter . . . exclusively. Federal jurisdiction comes into play only when LLC income tax returns are filed.

Since the formation of an LLC is a legal process, the question arises: Which state law? It is that state within which the LLC's principal place of business is intended to be conducted. It's the state of the "home office" of the LLC operation. Once formed in one state, a domestic LLC is reciprocally recognized in other states for legal and business purposes. Foreign LLCs, however, require separate registration in every separate state in which they operate.

For practical reasons and for instructional consistency, we need to select one set of LLC statutes (among the 51) on which to base our procedural discussions. We choose California. Since the 1960s, California has been the most populated state of the nation. It has a diversity of businesses: small, medium, large, and global. It has lots of laws . . . and lots of litigation. It enacted its *Limited Liability Company Act* on September 30, 1994. The Act is codified as Title 2.5 of the California Corporations Code (CCC).

Accordingly, in this chapter, based on California law, we want to step you through the formation and confirmation process of an LLC. Our focus is strictly on the legal aspects of the process, before ever filing any LLC tax returns. When particularly instructive, we'll cite specific sections of the 54,800-word California LLC law. We do this to impress on you that an LLC involves more legal technicalities than you may have been led to otherwise believe. If ever your personal liability as an LLC member is legally challenged, you and your colleagues must show good faith in compliance with all state laws under which your LLC is formed. Any material failure to do so could pierce that "limited liability" protective shield which you so fervently cherish.

Contact Secretary of State

For the state where you intend your LLC principal office to be, your first task is to contact that state's Secretary of State. All states have such an office in the capital city of its state. The functions of the Secretary of State are those of a law clerk and administrator for business filings, election matters, state archives, and certification of official documents. For procedural matters re LLCs, the Secretary of State is THE OFFICE to contact. You can do so by Internet, fax, phone, or mail. When you do, direct your inquiry to its *Limited Liability Company Unit*. If you are uncertain as to how best to make contact, phone the local office of your state's assembly member.

When making contact with your Secretary of State, what do you ask for? You ask for all pertinent forms, instructions, and fees for forming an LLC in your state. All you really want to know, initially, are the proper forms to file to legitimize your LLC. Large states like California will direct you to its website which is chock full of instructions and information. For example, California's Secretary of State's website will provide such documents as—

- Articles of Organization (for newly organized LLCs)
- Articles of Organization-Conversion (from a non-LLC)
- Amendment of Articles of Organization
- Restated Articles of Organization
- Statement of Information (re managers and owners)
- Designation of Agent for Service of Process
- Service of Process on LLC
- ... and so on

On the back of each LLC form, there are preprinted instructions. For example, on Form LLC-1: *Articles of Organization*, the instructions to Item 1 read, in part—

Enter the name of the limited liability company. The name shall contain the words "Limited Liability Company," or the abbreviations "LLC" or "L.L.C." as the last words in the name. The words "Limited" and "Company" may be abbreviated to "Ltd." and "Co.," respectively. ... (Section 17052).

Section 17052 is the applicable portion of the Limited Liability Company Act in the California Corporations Code. The express title of that section is: *Company name; recordation of instruments; effect.* In other words, the official LLC forms give you a synopsized version of what the state law is. For more specifics, you need to have access to the LLC law itself.

Your State's LLC Law

With or without like-minded colleagues, if you intend to form an LLC or to become a member of an existing one, prudence suggests that you acquire some familiarity with your state's LLC law. Sure, you could go to an attorney and have him or her guide you. But you'll not gain any "hands-on" knowledge this way. Attorneys, by training, are not very helpful in the exploratory, formulative, startup, and operational phases of a business. You'll need them later when binding contracts are required, and when litigative issues come up. For now, it is better that you do the paralegal research on your own.

In any manner that you can, get access to a complete copy of your state's LLC law. Search the web for legal sites and law book publishers. If frustration sets in, call the Law Librarian or Bar Association in the county where you reside. Ask for publisher references on law books that you can buy. Then write, phone, or e-mail the publisher for a compact edition (or an annotated edition with case citations) of LLC law. You want a printed and bound text in your hand that you can browse through and read and reference from time to time. Expect to pay $50 to $100 for such a text. You have no intention of becoming an LLC legal expert; you just want to become familiar first-hand, with what the law is all about. You need to have a full copy of it in your hands.

Browse through the LLC portion, and flag the content listing for each chapter. For example, California's LLC Chapter 2 is titled: *Formation*. Its chapter contents are listed as follows:

Section
17050 — Formation; requirements.
17051 — Articles of organization; contents.
17052 — Company name; recordation of instruments; effect.
17053 — Certificate of reservation of name; fee; issuance.
17054 — Amendment of articles of organization; filing; etc.
17055 — Certificate of correction; contents; execution; etc.
17056 — Execution of documents; resubmission; etc.
17057 — Maintenance of records; agent for legal service.
17058 — Information required to be maintained.
17059 — Operating agreement; power to adopt; alter; etc.
17060 — Statement of information.
17061 — Service of process.
17062 — Filing of instruments; date of filing.

There are 15 chapters of California LLC law. There is a total of 105 sections comprising approximately 54,800 words of text. Obviously, familiarity does not mean reading and memorizing every one of the 54,800 words. Some chapters can be glanced at and bypassed altogether. For example, the chapters on dissolution, foreign LLCs, class actions, conversions, and mergers are not of priority interest when forming and launching a newly organized domestic LLC. In contrast, those chapters on general provisions, members, management, finance, and so on, are vital to understanding the legal underpinnings of the LLC undertaking.

Go through and highlight those sections prescribing the general provisions and general limitations of an LLC. For example, under California law, Section 17050(b) states—

A limited liability company shall have one or more members.

Thus, in California, as in most other states, single member LLCs are permitted. The law, however, is written with multiple members in mind. No upper limit on number of members is specified. Depending on the type of business intended, and the amount of capital needed to run the business, there is some practical limit to every LLC membership. Each person who has a "capital interest" in the LLC (by contributing money, property, or services) is a part owner thereof. Having too many part owners, each with a voice in management, is just not going to work well.

What kind of business can your LLC engage in? Answer: California Section 17002: ***Business activity; limitations***, states—

*Subject to any limitations contained in the articles of organization and to compliance with other applicable laws, a limited liability company may engage in **any lawful business activity**, except the banking business, the business of issuing policies of insurance and assuming insurance risks, or the trust company business.* [Emphasis added.]

Except for the exceptions, "any lawful business activity" is quite broad. In fact, it is too broad. For practical reasons, every LLC should narrow its focus to some reasonably achievable business domain. Even though the law may imply so, you can't do everything. Common sense must prevail.

In Chapter 1, we described the unique flexibility of an LLC via three functional types of owner-member participation, namely: (1) material, (2) active, and (3) passive.

The Essence of Formation

Section 17050 of California LLC law is titled: *Formation; requirements.* Therein lies the essence of forming an LLC. Other states, we're sure, have identical (or nearly so) requirements. The Section 17050 (**a**) reads—

*In order to form a limited liability company, one or more persons shall execute and file articles of organization with, and on a form prescribed by, the Secretary of State and, either before or after the filing of the **articles of organization**, the members shall have entered into an **operating agreement**. The person or persons who execute and file the articles of organization may, but need not, be members of the limited liability company.* [Emphasis added.]

Note that two separate documents are required: (1) Articles of Organization, and (2) an Operating Agreement. Note that articles of organization are to be on a form prescribed by the Secretary of State. If you've followed our advice earlier, you would have in your hands such a form, or would have requested it. This form, in California, is designated as LLC-1: *Limited Liability Company; Articles of Organization.* We'll discuss the contents of this form, in full, shortly below.

Meanwhile, it is significant to note that there is no prescribed form for an operating agreement. Why? Because it is up to the LLC members themselves to prepare their own operating agreement form. This is what is meant by "either before or after" the filing of articles of organization . . . *the members shall have entered into an operating agreement.* At some point, therefore, all prospective members have to get together at an organizational meeting and agree on the elements of their modus operandi.

Our position is that prospective members should get together **before** filing articles of organization. They need to thrash out among themselves the pros and cons of an LLC; the general provisions and limitations of their state's LLC law; the extent and content of its official forms; the type of business (or businesses) they propose to get into; the initial amount of capital needed; whether or not "certificates of membership" will be issued; the assignment of managerial tasks; the outlining of voting procedures and rights; the designation of books, records, and accounts to be kept; the selection of a company name; and so on. We depict in Figure 2.1 what some of the agenda items might be, for constituting an organizational meeting.

The meeting should be conducted in a business-like manner. Minutes should be taken and printed up for subsequent distribution to all attendants. The "meeting" may consist of two, three, or more consecutive sessions and still be classed as an organizational meeting. The objective should be: (1) an *outline* of the operating agreement; (2) a tentative decision on a company name; and (3) the designation of an "organizer" who is to prepare, execute, file, and advance the filing fee for the Articles of Organization. The organizer should be one of the attendants at the meeting.

Note that we say a "tentative" decision on a company name. As per Section 17052(c), the name—

> *Shall not be a name that the Secretary of State determines is likely to mislead the public and shall not be the same as, or resemble so closely as to tend to deceive the name of any LLC that has filed articles of organization . . ., or any name that is under reservation for another LLC.*

Section 17053 specifies that—

> *Any applicant may, upon payment of the fee prescribed . . ., obtain from the Secretary of State a certificate of reservation of any name not prohibited . . . for a period of 60 days.*

The point we are making is that any member-agreed company name is only tentative. It is so until the Secretary of State accepts it and reserves it by issuing a certificate. You want to nail down your LLC name before actually filing its articles of organization.

Articles of Organization; Contents

The legitimacy of an LLC is affirmed by the filing of its Articles of Organization, and the acceptance of them by the Secretary of State. This is the function of the designated

"Organizer" listed in Figure 2.1. Also indicated are other subjects for discussion.

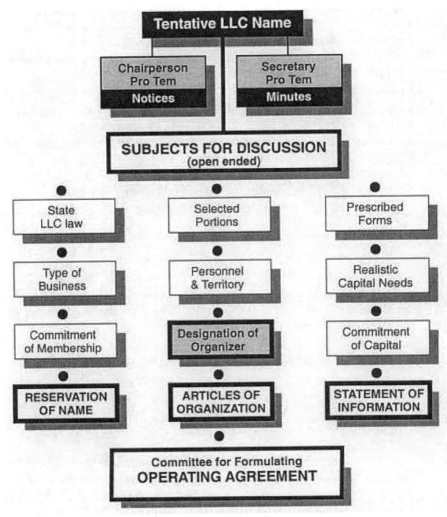

Fig. 2.1 - LLC Meeting for Preliminary Discussion & Concensus

In California, the law on point is Section 17050(**c**). This section reads—

The existence of a limited liability company begins upon the filing of the articles of organization. For all purposes, a copy *of the articles of organization duly certified by the Secretary of State is **conclusive evidence** of the formation of a limited liability company and prima facie evidence of its existence.*

Section 17051 outlines the contents of the Articles document: name, purpose, type of business, management, termination, agent for service, etc. In California, all of the statutory content required is preprinted on its Form LLC-1 (cited earlier). This official form is self-explanatory, especially after reading its instructions on the back. A bold headnote there says—

DO NOT ALTER THIS FORM
Type or legibly print in black ink.

If other information is to be provided, it is to be made on separate pages. Because this adds clutter to a one-page official document, rarely are other pages attached. The executed form itself, plus a $70 filing fee, is all that California wants.

If you intend to become an LLC in a state that does not provide a preprinted Articles of Organization form, request its Secretary of State to provide you with a sample of what it wants. At least ask for its statutory requirements so that you (with an attorney) can make up your own form. Chances are, the state bar association will have developed preprinted/approval forms for such purpose.

Because the California Form LLC-1 is statutorily complete, instead of going through its contents item by item, we present a condensed version of it in Figure 2.2. Note that in the upper right-hand corner, there is blank space for entering a **File #**_____. Once assigned, this number is used on all correspondence and filings between the LLC and the Secretary of State. Do not confuse this number with any Tax ID (Federal or State) that must be used when filing tax returns.

Item 3 in Figure 2.2 requires that either the name of an individual, or the name of a corporation, be entered as the Agent for Service of (legal) Process. Often this is an attorney or legal firm, though it could be any designated member of the LLC. This is your tip-off that being an LLC does not exonerate the LLC or its members from litigative actions. Thus, a designated agent for the acceptance of service of legal papers must be available at all times.

	State of California Secretary of State • LIMITED LIABILITY COMPANY ARTICLES OF ORGANIZATION	File # _____ ┌ Space for ┐ State └ Certification ┘
STATE SEAL Filing Fee $____		

1.	ENTITY NAME
2.	PURPOSE: To engage in any lawful act or activity... (all preprinted; no changes allowed)
3.	INITIAL AGENT for service of process: ☐ Individual ☐ Corporation
4.	California Address of Agent: _____
5.	MANAGEMENT: (check one) ☐ one manager ☐ more than one manager ☐ single member LLC ☐ all LLC members
6.	ADDITIONAL INFORMATION: Other matters to be included. May include type of business, and expected date of dissolution. Attach separate pages.
7.	EXECUTION: Declaration by person who executes instrument. ____ Signature of Organizer ____ ____ Type or Print Name ____ Date: _____
8.	RETURN TO: Name Company Address

Sec/State Form LLC-1

Fig. 2.2 - Condensed Version of California "Prescribed" Form LLC-1

Item 6 permits other matters to be set forth on separate pages, to be made part of the certification process. The instructions encourage the inclusion of the latest date or event on which the LLC is to dissolve. The implication is that an LLC shall not have indefinite life, like that of a corporation.

Item 7 is a Declaration by the Organizer who is executing and signing the Articles of Organization. The instructions stress that only an *original signature* (not a facsimile) is acceptable by the Secretary of State. As indicated previously in Section 17050(a), the signature of the organizer need not be that of a member or manager of the LLC. However, our position is that the organizer should be an LLC member. Otherwise, the LLC loses touch with reality when it relies too heavily on nonmembers for legal tasks. An agent is one thing; an organizer is closer to home.

Statement of Information

Within 90 days after the filing of Articles of Organization, California law requires the filing of a statement of information *on a form prescribed by the Secretary of State.* Said prescribed document is **Form LLC-12**: *Limited Liability Company: Statement of Information.* As with the LLC-1, self-explanatory instructions are on the back of Form LLC-12. The leadoff instructions tell you that said form is required biennially (every two years) after its initial filing.

The primary purpose of the Statement of Information is to keep the Secretary of State's LLC files up to date with respect to the—

1. Agent for service of process,
2. Principal business activity,
3. Office(s) for maintenance of records, and
4. Names and addresses of all members, managers, and CEOs (if any) . . . on attached pages (as necessary).

Persons authorized to execute and sign Form LLC-12 "shall be" any manager (or CEO), attorney in fact, or any member designated by majority vote of the LLC governing body. The declarant (executing agent) attests that—

This statement is true, correct, and complete.

By innuendo in the instructions to Form LLC-12, the declaration of truthfulness and completeness includes Section 17057: *Offices for maintenance of records.* This section reads—

*Each limited liability company **shall continuously maintain** in this state* [California] *each of the following:*

*(a) An office at which shall be maintained the records required by **Section 17058**.*

(b) An agent in this state for service of process on the limited liability company. [Emphasis added.]

We're not sure that you sense the legal significance of what we've just presented to you. If not, we depict in Figure 2.3 what we believe to be the jugular vein of an LLC operation. Like any business entity, an LLC **is subject to** litigative attack by any customer, supplier, lender, or member who becomes disgruntled or dissatisfied in his/her/its dealings with the LLC entity. A reasonable cause would exist if there is any failure to comply with ALL of the elements of Section 17058 (of California law).

Information Required to be Maintained

Section 17058 is titled: ***Information required to be maintained at office***. The term "at office" means the principal, head, home, or central office of the LLC. If the required information is scattered among various members, managers, and agents, the arrangement would be "out-of-sync" with the statutory requirement for California. We are sure that other states would insist similarly.

Because of the importance of Section 17058, we want to cite it, essentially in full. It reads (with emphasis added)—

*(a) Each limited liability company shall maintain at the office . . . **all of** the following:*

> *(1) A current list of the full name and last known business or residence address of each member and of each holder of an economic interest in the LLC set forth in alphabetical order, together with the contribution and the share in profits and losses of each member and holder of an economic interest.*

> *(2) A current list of the full name and business or residence address of each manager.*

> *(3) A copy of the articles of organization and **all amendments thereto**, together with any powers of*

attorney pursuant to which the articles of organization or any amendments thereto were executed.

Fig. 2.3 - Potential Litigants If Mandated Records Not Maintained

*(4)   Copies of the LLC's **federal, state, and local income tax or information returns** and reports, if any, for the **six most recent taxable years**.*

(5)   A copy of the LLC's operating agreement, if in writing, and any amendments thereto . . .

*(6)   Copies of the **financial statements** of the LLC, if any, for the six most recent fiscal years.*

*(7)   The books and records of the LLC as they relate to the **internal affairs** of the company for at least the current and past four fiscal years.*

*(b)   Upon request of an Assessor, a domestic or foreign LLC owning, claiming, possessing, or controlling **property** in this state **subject to local assessment** shall make available . . . at the office required . . . or at a place mutually acceptable to the Assessor and the LLC, a true copy of business records relevant to the amount, cost, and value of all property that it owns, claims, possesses, or controls within the county.*

The tracking, preparing, posting, and maintaining the above information — **continuously** — is a tall order. It is daunting and burdensome to an LLC whose members are cavalier, procrastinative, and indifferent to recordkeeping chores. This characteristic alone justifies the need for an explicit Operating Agreement . . . IN WRITING. Note that paragraph 17058(a)(5) above refers to such agreement as: *if in writing*. If not in writing, can't you see the finger pointing among members when responsibility questions arise, finances are low, and assets are dispersed. This is reckless exposure of your jugular vein, when legal adversaries start their drum beat and war dance.

Operating Agreement: A "Must"

Of the 105 sections of California LLC law (2005 version), only Section 17059 addresses directly the issue of an operating agreement. This is a two-sentence section comprising 46 words only. Its gist is succinctly stated in its title: *Operating agreement; power to adopt, alter, amend, or repeal; procedures*. Its first sentence reads—

*The power to adopt, alter, amend, or repeal the operating agreement of a limited liability company **shall be vested** in the members. [Emphasis added.]*

Note that no power to adopt an operating agreement is vested in an organizer, manager, agent, attorney, or other person who is not a member of the LLC. Only bona fide members (those who contribute capital) have the power to adopt, alter, amend, repeal . . . etc. It is significant to further note that the statutory wording does **not** say: "shall adopt." The wording only says: "power to adopt." So, why not use such power?

The second sentence of Section 17059 reads—

*The articles of organization **or a written** operating agreement **may prescribe** the manner in which the operating agreement may be altered, amended, or repealed.* [Emphasis added.]

This does not tell us very much other than that a written operating agreement is included in the power to adopt. But, what is an "operating agreement"? What happens if the LLC members fail to adopt an operating agreement in writing?

California Section 17001(ab) defines such an instrument as—

*Any agreement, **written or oral**, between **all** the members as to the affairs of a limited liability company and the conduct of its business in any manner not inconsistent with law or the articles of organization. . . .The term "operating agreement" may include, **without more**, an agreement between all members to organize a limited liability company pursuant to the provisions of this title* [Title 2.5: Limited Liability Companies; California Corporations Code]. [Emphasis added.]

Here's the answer to our question about failure to adopt a written operating agreement. Members may agree orally — or, they may agree *silently* — not to have such an instrument. If they so agree (not to have), they expose themselves to mandatory compliance with each and every item of the 54,800-word CCC Title 2.5! This is a legal doctrine of long standing. When given an opportunity to do something, and the response is silence, the silence is construed to mean consent to the "maximum provisions" imposed by law.

Consequently, we cannot urge too strongly that a written operating agreement be adopted by LLC members. It need not be

THE PROS & CONS OF LLCs

an elaborate document. But it does need to cover the relationships between members themselves, between members and the LLC, and between the LLC and the public at large (particularly customers, suppliers, and lenders). The instrument should also include the assignment of tasks, capital requirements, recordkeeping, financial statements, tax returns, and other internal affairs which are characteristic of a well-run enterprise. For other thoughts, you may study our Figure 2.4.

Unlike the Articles of Organization, for which no attorney is necessary, we urge that you do engage an attorney. Engage one who is knowledgeable in LLC case law for your state, and who will not draft an instrument that is too sophisticated or too obfuscative to be comprehended fully by all members. Think of the instrument as a binding contract between serious members who intend to engage in business seriously.

Cash Starvation by Members

There is one critical area where an operating agreement can prove its worth. It concerns capital contributions to, shortages of, and withdrawals from company assets. Virtually every small- and medium-sized business tends to be capital starved. An LLC, with members who are fascinated with misconceptions of the limited liability concept, is particularly susceptible to the cash starvation process. A responsibly adopted operating agreement can forestall — and possibly prevent — the premature termination of an enterprise based on capital deficiencies alone. On this premise, California LLC Sections 17200 and 17201 are instructive.

Section 17200: *Capital contributions,* reads in part—

The operating agreement may provide for capital contributions of members. [Such contributions] *may be in money, property, or services, or* ***other obligation*** *to contribute money or property or to render services.* [Emphasis added.]

Note in the foregoing citation the term: "obligation to . . .". Said obligation is spelled out expressly in Section 17201: ***Obligation to contribute cash, property, or services*** (etc.). This section reads in part—

2-16

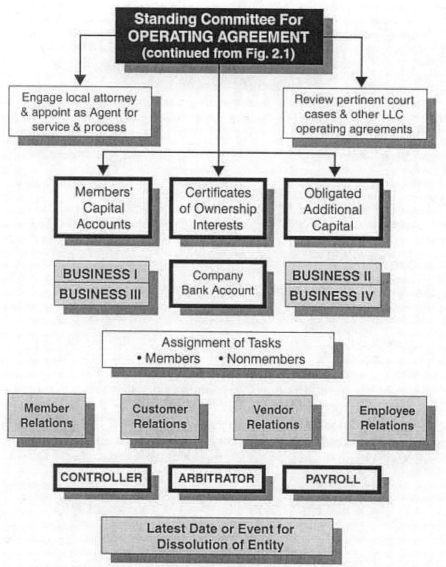

Fig. 2.4 - Indicators of the Seriousness (and Continuity) of LLC Effort

*Subject to the terms of the operating agreement, a member is **not excused** from an obligation . . . to perform any promise to contribute cash or property or to perform services because of death, disability, dissolution, or any other reason. . . . An*

operating agreement may provide that the [ownership] *interest of a member who fails to make any contributions or other payment that the member is required to make **will be subject to specific remedies for,** or specific consequences of, the failure. . . . The specific remedies or consequences may include loss of voting, approval, or other rights, loss of the member's ability to participate in the management and operations of the company, liquidated damages, or **a reduction of** the defaulting member's **economic rights**.*

In other words, an LLC has the power to financially discipline its own members. Failure to do so, when economic prudence requires, could be construed as prima facie evidence that the LLC is functioning as a sham.

Section 17003: ***Powers in carrying out business activities***, lists 20 paragraphs of specific LLC powers (subsections (a) through (t)). For example, subsection (d) states that an LLC has the power to—

make contracts and guarantees, incur liabilities, act as surety [be responsible for its members], *and borrow money.*

Can't you sense the flood of legal actions against your LLC should it exercise its business powers without obligating all members to come forth financially? Of all the opportunistic features of an LLC, we think that failure to obligate members to maintain an adequate capital base is an LLC's most vulnerable weakness.

3

LIABILITY OF MEMBERS

Every LLC Member Can Expect Protection Against Personal Liability IF, AND ONLY IF, Certain Conditions Are Met. Among These Are: (1) Maintaining One's Agreed Share Of The LLC's Capital Base; (2) Separating, Totally, Entity Activities From Personal Activities (Otherwise, There Is ALTER EGO LIABILITY); (3) Carrying One's Load For Accuracy Of Books And Records, Including The Operating Agreement; And (4) Avoiding All Tortious Conduct (Breach Of Duty) Towards Customers And Creditors. If So Stated In The Operating Agreement, Any Member May Separately Insure Himself Against The Misdeeds Of Other Members.

There is a misconception, widely held, that by merely forming an LLC, every member thereof is insulated from all personal liability to third-party plaintiffs. This is definitely not the case. True, there is some protection against such liability **but only if** certain statutory conditions are met. The conditions are prescribed by state law, but even then the protection is limited to the extent of each member's economic interest in the LLC activity as a whole. In other words, if a member's economic interest in the LLC is $10,000, he can be held liable up to that amount . . . under most circumstances.

However, if a member engages in breach of contract, tortious acts (fraud or misrepresentation), failure to maintain his capital obligations to the LLC, or does other acts in violation of state law, no protection is afforded. The protective LLC shield is legally pierced. In this event, the member or members can be held personally liable for what might otherwise be the debts and obligations of the LLC.

The purpose of the LLC statute for the state in which you do business is to establish the compliance rules for an effective legal shield. The rules, of course, will differ from state to state. Nevertheless, the rules boil down basically to keeping certain records, maintaining adequate capital reserves, honoring contractual commitments, avoiding tortious acts, and following formalities comparable to those of a well-run corporation.

Accordingly, in this chapter, we want to continue with California law. We particularly want to focus on those statutory provisions which we think would be used foremost against you, in litigative action for probable cause. There is no better place to start than that section of California LLC law subheaded: *Liability of members* (Section 17101).

The Basic Protection Rule

Subsection (**a**) of Section 17101 provides that—

Except as provided in Section 17254 or subsection (e), **no member** *of a limited liability company* **shall be personally liable** *under any judgment of a court, or in any other manner,* **for any debt, obligation, or liability of the limited liability company,** *whether that liability or obligation arises in contract, tort, or otherwise,* **solely by reason of being** *a member of the limited liability company.* [Emphasis added.]

Except for the two exceptions, what does Section 17101(a) say? It says — between the lines — that if you as an LLC member have "deep pockets," and the LLC as an entity does not, you are protected. The mere fact that you are a member of the LLC and the fact that the LLC incurred a liability exceeding its asset and capital base, you cannot be held liable beyond your share of that base. This, at least, is a valid affirmative defense should the plaintiff establish (with credible evidence) that the LLC was run carelessly and imprudently, or violated some other law. As the deep pockets member, always keep your capital account positive.

The legal theory here is *separable liability*. This contrasts with joint and several liability, such as in a partnership or joint venture. Consequently, separable liability is the key on which Section 17101 is premised, and on which the concept of limited liability rests. Because of its fundamental importance, we depict the separability concept for you in Figure 3.1.

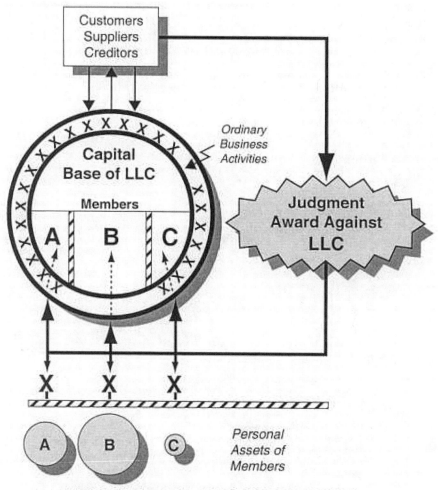

Fig. 3.1 - The Separable Liability Concept of an LLC

Let us illustrate Figure 3.1 with simple numbers. You are one of three members in an LLC. As member "A" you have a 30%

ownership interest which represents $50,000 of the LLC's capital base. The LLC is sued for some cause whereupon the plaintiff is awarded a $100,000 judgment. Your share of that judgment is $30,000 ($100,000 x 30%). It is not the full $50,000 of your economic interest in the LLC. This is because the plaintiff will get $50,000 from member "B" ($100,000 x 50%) and $20,000 from member "C" ($100,000 x 20%). The presumption here is that each member diligently maintains in the LLC his prorata capital base.

Instead, now, suppose your 30% interest represents $25,000 of the LLC's capital base. The plaintiff, again, is awarded $100,000 against the LLC. Arithmetically, your share of the liability is $30,000. But the plaintiff can only collect $25,000 from the LLC for your part. Can the plaintiff go after you personally for the $5,000 liability deficiency on your part?

Technically, No. But he will try. Knowing how aggressive trial attorneys can be, the plaintiff's attorney will hammer away at the LLC shield until some tiny pinhole appears.

The "Prohibited Distribution" Rule

How can a trial attorney pierce the LLC shield when you are protected by Section 17101(a)?

Answer: This is where the first exception to Section 17101(a) comes in. Recall that its opening clause reads— *Except as otherwise provided in Section 17254. . . .* What is this cross-reference all about?

Section 17254 is titled: ***Prohibited distributions***, etc. Its subsection (a) states primarily that—

*No distribution shall be made if, after giving effect to the distribution, **either** of the following occurs:*

*(1) The LLC would **not be able to pay its debts** as they become due in the normal course of business.*

*(2) The LLC's total assets would be less than **the sum of its total liabilities** plus . . . the amount that would be needed, if the LLC were to be dissolved at the time of the distribution. . . .* [Emphasis added.]

Let's go back to the $100,000 judgment liability example above. Suppose that shortly after the lawsuit was filed, you, as a 30% member, requested a distribution of $25,000 of your $50,000 capital base in the LLC. The 50% member agreed; the 20% member disagreed. After your drawdown, the company was left with enough assets to pay its ordinary debts when due [paragraph (1) above]. Now, what?

As per paragraph (2) above, your $25,000 distribution caused the company assets to fall below its total liabilities when including the $100,000 judgment. Knowing that a lawsuit had been filed, your request constitutes negligence and impropriety. Thus, you will be liable for your full 30% share of the judgment.

Now, suppose the 50% member demands distribution of his entire capital base in the LLC (around $85,000). You and the 20% member vehemently disagree. The 50% member becomes violent, pounds the table, and threatens a counter lawsuit against both of you. Reluctantly — and nervously — you both agree. Each of you has left all of your initial capital base in the LLC (totaling also around $85,000). The judgment and ordinary debts are expected to total about $150,000. Are you and your 20% colleague LLC protected? You thought so, didn't you?

Surprise! You both have compounded your negligence and impropriety. As a result, you both are treated as partners ex parte (outside of the LLC). You both now are jointly and severally liable for the $100,000 judgment *and* for the approximately $50,000 of ordinary LLC debt. The plaintiff and creditor(s) can collect from either of you or from both of you. When a matter is statutorily prohibited, as Section 17254 says, and you violate that prohibition, the LLC shield provides no protection whatsoever.

The "Agree to be Obligated" Rule

There's a second exception to the basic LLC protection rule. It is subsection (e) of Section 17101 as cross-referenced above. The subsection (e) reads—

*Notwithstanding subsection (a), **a member** of an LLC **may agree to be obligated personally for any or all** of the debts, obligations, and liabilities of the LLC as long as the agreement* *to be so obligated is set forth . . . in a written operating agreement that specifically references this subsection.* [Emphasis added.]

Why would a member *agree to be obligated* for any or all of an LLC's debts and liabilities? There are valid reasons.

Note that Section 17101(e) says "a" member. It does not say "all" members. Also note that the personal liability assumed may apply to "**any** or all" of the LLC's obligation. We're not sure of the legal interpretation of these items. Ordinary reasoning suggests that if one member assumed a specific obligation beyond his required capital base, he has insulated himself from other extraneous matters, should other members of the LLC engage in improper acts. The stark reality is that the "LL" shield alone does not protect a dutiful member from those who are cavalier.

It is beyond us why any one member would obligate himself for all of the debts and liabilities of a multi-member LLC. If other members appear to be irresponsible in their business duties, why carry the load for all? However, if it is a two-member LLC, and one member is not carrying his load, the responsible member could assume all obligations and "vote out" the non-performing member.

Every LLC is supposed to have a capital base sufficient to cover all ordinary debts when due, plus the cost of dissolution. When there are three or more members in an LLC that is chronically "cash short," a more prudent member might agree to obligate himself for his share of any lawsuits that might arise. No matter how justified a lawsuit might be, the settlement time and judgment award are difficult to predict. Rather than worrying about collateral liability based on some quirky technicality, a member might obligate himself in advance. By doing so in writing (in the LLC's operating agreement), he can set the terms and conditions for his added obligation. Presumably, such could stave off any unconscionable lawsuit against that member. Presumably, also, the LLC protection shield would hold for that member.

The "Shall Carry Insurance" Rule

There is another statutory rule that further defines the degree of legal protection that an LLC affords. The applicable rule is subsection (d) of Section 17101. We call it the "shall carry insurance" rule. Subsection (d) reads as—

> *An LLC . . . shall carry insurance **or provide an undertaking to the same extent** and in the same amount as is required by law, rule, or regulation of this state that would be applicable to the company . . . **were it a corporation** . . . duly qualified for the transaction of intrastate business under the General Corporation Law* [of California]. [Emphasis added.]

This is not a particularly definitive requirement. We think it invites lawsuit because of its lack of specifying an overall amount (such as a percentage of gross sales), and its lack of identifying specific coverage(s). How much, and what type of insurance is adequate for an LLC? Can't you see a trial lawyer probing this matter to threads?

If there is no insurance at all carried by the LLC, you can be sure that this would be one of the causes of action in a lawsuit. Even if the defense were "an undertaking to the same extent" (as insurance), it would be a hard sell in court.

One equivalent undertaking that would likely be accepted is the "agreement to obligate" provision in subsection (e) above. Another equivalent undertaking would be a disciplinary provision in the operating agreement requiring personal liability insurance by each capital-deficient member. The insurance would be purchased and paid for by each deficient member, naming the LLC as the beneficiary of the proceeds. A nominal face-amount policy, such as $100,000, should be prescribed by the disciplinary agreement.

What is the guideline if none of the equivalent measures above is acceptable to LLC members? In this case, the manager must undertake a survey of the insurance coverage by those businesses similar to his, which are in corporate form. This is smart for two reasons. One, you cover the intent of law. And, secondly, the competitive premium rates would likely be lower for corporations than for a fully exposed LLC. Our contention is that, by being an LLC, insurers are likely to "pad" their rates. Especially so if it appears that some members consider the limited liability shield itself as being a form of insurance. Indeed, many LLC participants decline to carry any form of liability insurance in the belief that their LLC status gives them all the legal protection they need. We are sorry to have to cast cold water on any such delusion(s).

The "Alter Ego Liability" Rule

The doctrine of alter ego liability is one of long standing. It has evolved from the many abuses of closely-held entities, such as corporations, partnerships, and trusts. And, now, closely-held LLCs. The term "closely held" means five or fewer individuals owning 50% or more of the controlling interests of an entity. In these situations, the distinction between entity business and personal business is blurred and commingled. To invoke the alter ego doctrine, it has to be shown that the entity was a mere conduit for the transaction of personal business and that no separate identity of the individual and the entity really existed.

The lack of separate identity stands out starkly when there is commingling of funds, disguising of expenditures, unrestrained drawdown of capital, poor recordkeeping, lavish travel and entertainment, and the like. Owner self-discipline in separating business from personal matters is minimal or nonexistent. The entity formulation and use of its registered name is an "ego thing" for the close owners.

Section 17101(**b**) does not exonerate LLC members from alter ego liability. To the contrary, it expressly states—

*A member of an LLC **shall be subject** to liability under the common law governing alter ego liability, **and shall also** be personally liable under a judgment of a court **or for** any debt, obligation, or liability of the LLC, whether that liability or obligation arises in contract, tort, or otherwise, **under the same or similar circumstances** and to the same extent **as a shareholder of a corporation** may be personally liable.* [Emphasis added.]

There is no wiggle room here. Once it can be shown that there is no distinct line of separation between the entity and one or more of its members, each such member becomes subject to personal liability. It is the de facto act or acts that count legally. For example, the operating agreement prohibits any personal transactions on company letterhead, writing company checks, or using company equipment. Nevertheless, some senior member goes ahead and makes his monthly mortgage payments on his personal home with company checks. Doing so, he has snagged the trip wire into alter ego liability. So important is this doctrine that we depict it the best we can in Figure 3.2.

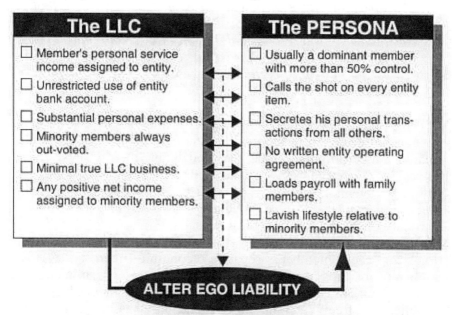

The LLC

☐ Member's personal service income assigned to entity.

☐ Unrestricted use of entity bank account.

☐ Substantial personal expenses.

☐ Minority members always out-voted.

☐ Minimal true LLC business.

☐ Any positive net income assigned to minority members.

The PERSONA

☐ Usually a dominant member with more than 50% control.

☐ Calls the shot on every entity item.

☐ Secretes his personal transactions from all others.

☐ No written entity operating agreement.

☐ Loads payroll with family members.

☐ Lavish lifestyle relative to minority members.

ALTER EGO LIABILITY

Fig. 3.2 - Elements of Indistinguishability Between Entity and Persona

It is important to be aware that if one member acquires alter ego liability, he carries his burden alone. Other members are unaffected unless they, too, ignore the separability doctrine of Figure 3.1

The "Like-a-Corporation" Standard

If you survive the separability doctrine, there are other LLC technicalities which could subject a member or members to personal liability. Most such technicalities are comparable to those of a corporation. Indeed, many LLCs structure their internal affairs "like a corporation" without the strict formalities of a corporation. The most likely first attack on this front would be the

THE PROS & CONS OF LLCs

operating agreement. This instrument, functionally, is much like that of the rules and by-laws of a corporation. If an LLC truly wants legal protection, it has to act responsibly.

As a starter, California's LLC Section 17105(a): ***Certificate of interest*** (etc.) says—

> *The operating agreement may provide that the interest of a member or assignee in an LLC may be evidenced by a certificate of interest issued by the LLC, and make other provisions . . . with respect to the transfer of interests represented by those certificates or with respect to the form of those certificates.*

The idea of issuing "certificates of interest" representing a member's ownership in the business closely resembles the idea of shares in a corporation. True, the cited statute merely says: "*may* provide." Nevertheless, you should always count on a plaintiff's attorney demanding a copy of an LLC's operating agreement. Such a demand — called: *right of discovery* — will almost certainly open up a can of legal worms.

If no certificates of interest are issued, how does the LLC keep track of each member's separate economic interests? How meticulously are capital account records kept? Can members switch their interests back and forth among themselves and families, or freely among close friends and associates? How reliable and updated is the transactional accounting on these matters? If the operating agreement is too flexible, too unspecific, or too silent on these matters, the alter ego liability doctrine comes back into play.

A favored target for probing the adequacy of the operating agreement is Section 17202: ***Profits and losses; allocation among members***. This "shall be" section reads—

> *The profits and losses of an LLC **shall be allocated** among the members, and among classes of members, in the manner provided in the operating agreement. If the operating agreement does not otherwise provide, profits and losses shall be allocated **in proportion to the contributions** of each member.* [Emphasis added.]

The term "contributions" refers to the amount of money, property, and after-tax services that are dedicated irrevocably to the LLC entity, in exchange for economic interests therein.

Here's the classical legal quagmire that arises from capital accounting issues. As of on or about a certain date (of alleged misconduct), were the accounts posted prior — or subsequent — to the cause of action date? If made prior (which is good) were they made by a person of knowledge who had a duty to make the entries in a timely manner. Trying to doctor up records after a lawsuit is filed is clear admission of fault.

Retroactive Corrections Preempted

When the lawsuits against an LLC start, a flaying of finger pointing goes around. Defensive members become avid record correctors. They work feverishly to clear out adverse commentary; they substitute "corrected" versions; and they add missing or overlooked items. Those who have agreed to take on management tasks hurriedly prepare their job descriptions. The whole effort is to tighten up, retroactively, what has been a loosely run LLC.

California LLC Section 17157 preempts any retroactive reshuffling of records affecting manager and agent responsibilities. The section is titled: ***Agents of the company for purposes of transacting business or affairs***. Its subsection (a) reads—

> ***Unless*** *the statement referred to in subsection (b) of Section 17151* [re Management by one or more managers] *is included in the **articles of organization**, every member is an agent of the LLC for the purpose of its business or affairs, and the **act of any member** . . . for the apparent purpose of carrying on in the usual way the business or affairs of the LLC . . . **binds the LLC**, unless the member so acting has in fact no authority to act for the LLC in the particular matter, and the person with whom the member is dealing has actual knowledge of the fact that the member has no such authority.* [Emphasis added.]

Can't you see? Any after-the-fact designation of managers and delegation of authority pertaining to business and operating affairs is too late.   Unless the Articles of Organization — *not* the operating agreement — provide for the management aspects of the LLC, the act or acts of every member can bind the company. Therefore, you need to know about the "Unless" clause referenced in the citation above.   That reference, recall, is subsection (b) of Section 17151.

Subsection (b) of Section 17151:   ***Management*** (etc.) reads primarily as—

> *If the LLC is to be managed by one or more managers and not by all its members, the articles of organization shall contain a statement to that effect . . . but if management is vested in only one manager, the articles of organization shall so state.*

As pointed out in the preceding chapter, California provides a prescribed form for an LLC's ***Articles of Organization*** [recall Figure 2.2 on page 2-10].   Item 5 of that form calls to your attention the management issue.   That item reads expressly as—

> *The limited liability company will be managed by: (**check one**)*

☐ one manager   ☐ more than one manager
☐ all limited liability company members
☐ single member limited liability company

In other words, you have to commit your management arrangement up-front: not after-the-fact.   Of course, you can always amend the Articles . . . and notify the Secretary of State when you do.

Outsourced Management Permitted

If provision is made in the Articles of Organization for management by other than all members, three benefits accrue. One, the manager or managers need not be a member of the LLC [Subsec. 17151(**a**)].   Two, the manager or managers need not be a natural person [Subsec. 17151(**c**)].   A partnership, corporation, or trust could be a manager.   And, three, once management is vested in a manager or managers outside of the LLC, then—

No member, acting solely in the capacity of a member, is an agent of the LLC, nor can any member bind, nor execute any instrument on behalf of, the LLC [Subsec. 17157(b)(1)].

This sounds to us as if the outsourcing of management responsibilities of an LLC could be an advantageous way to go. Though clearly permitted by California law (and, presumably, by other states as well), whether your LLC does so or not depends on the potential for personal liability by various members. Those members or prospective members who have substantial personal assets may not want to expose those assets to the unknowns of a new or converted LLC. In such case, the idea of a Management Contract with qualified nonmembers might be appealing.

A management contract with nonmember managers would have to be an independent document of its own. It should be independent of both the Articles of Organization and the Operating Agreement. However, because the operating agreement is empowered by the members of the LLC (not by the Secretary of State), any decision on management policy should be set forth initially in the operating agreement. After proper proposal, discussion, and resolution by a majority of the voting member interests, an outsourced management contract can be put forth. When legally complete, such a contract can be appendaged to the operating agreement and made a part thereof, by reference. As a separate contract between the LLC and its chosen management firm, the contract is subject to litigative enforcement independent of the internal affairs of the LLC itself.

Before deciding on an outsourcing management contract, certain statutory items should be brought to the attention of all LLC members. For one, there are fiduciary duties and responsibilities of a trusted manager or managers. On this, California LLC Section 17153: **Fiduciary duties**, states—

The fiduciary duties a manager owes to the LLC and to its members are those of a partner to a partnership and to the partners of the partnership.

In other words, an outsourced manager or management firm is like a general partner in a partnership consisting of the manager (a management firm) and the LLC. This *implies* a joint and several liability relationship. Statutorily, however, outsourced managers must be extended conditional immunity from personal liability by the LLC. The relevant portion of California law here is Section 17158: *Immunity of managers*. Its statutory wording is—

> *No person who is a **manager or officer** or both a manager and officer of an LLC **shall be personally liable** under any judgment of a court, or in any other manner, for any debt, obligation or liability of the LLC, whether that liability arises in contract, tort, or otherwise, **solely by reason** of being a manager or officer or both a manager and officer of the LLC.* [Emphasis added.]

In other respects, Section 17155 has particular significance of its own. Its full title is: *Indemnification of managers, members, officers, employees, or agents; insurance*. The gist here is that the operating agreement of an LLC—

> *may provide for the indemnification of any person, including without limitation, any manager, member, officer, employee, or agent of the LLC, against judgments, settlements, penalties, fines, or expenses of any kind incurred as a result of acting in that capacity. The LLC shall have the power to purchase and maintain insurance on behalf of any* [person above].

We try to summarize the above for you in Figure 3.3. Until the management contract is either canceled or altered materially, the managers "run the show." The members function as a board of directors for policy and financial control. To assure smooth functioning between managers and owners, the management contract (between owners and managers) **and** the operating agreement (between the members themselves) should be reviewed periodically.

No Shield for Tortious Conduct

The term "tortious" means: *of or involving a tort*. The term "tort" means: *a wrongful act, injury, or damage (not involving breach of contract) for which civil action can be brought.* These are the definitions we find in an ordinary dictionary.

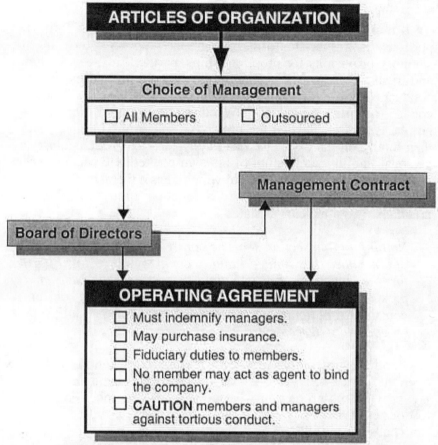

Fig. 3.3 - Features of an LLC With Outsourced Management

More specifically, tort is a legal term that covers a variety of harmful behavior. Considered "harmful" or "wrongful" is a breach of that behavior which exists by virtue of **society's expectation** regarding interpersonal conduct. Society does not expect one person to harm another person: his body, his property, his economic interests, his reputation, his privacy, his "whatever." Tort is the interference with someone else's right to life, liberty, and the pursuit of happiness. A tortious act is that which takes place beyond contract law, and that which creeps up on criminal law. Tort law is not well codified because it covers that amorphous span of human interaction known as: "common law."

What's our point here?

It is that LLC law, of which we have cited selected California portions, is a specific form of contract law. So, too, are the statutory provisions for proprietorships, partnerships, corporations, and trusts. None of these contract-law provisions address tortious conduct. Consequently, our point is that if an LLC member engages in tortious conduct — whether knowingly or otherwise — he places himself *beyond* the protective shield of LLC law. He is then totally on his own. He has to pay for and insure against any personal liability actions out of his own pocket. He cannot expect indemnification from the LLC of which he is a member.

On this point, subsection (c) of Section 17101: ***Liability of members***, is quite clear. It states—

Nothing in this section shall be construed to affect the liability of a member of a limited liability company (1) to third parties for the member's participation in tortious conduct, or (2) pursuant to the terms of a written guarantee or other contractual obligation entered into by the member, other than an operating agreement.

In other words, other than via a specific provision in the LLC's operating agreement — to which all members must agree — LLC law provides no protection whatsoever to any member engaged in tortious conduct.

That's our point!

4

IRS ELECTION FORM 8832

An Eligible Entity May Elect To Be Income Taxed As A Corporation, A Partnership, Or A Proprietorship. An "Eligible Entity" Is Any Arrangement Of Entrepreneurial Interests Not Statutorily Mandated To Be A Corporation. The Election Option Is Available To Any Group Of Associates, Whether An LLC Or Not. Selecting An Entity Name And Formulating Its Operational Characteristics Are Prerequisites. A "60-Month Rule" Discourages "Tax Whipsawing" And "Debt Whipsawing" By Limiting The Frequency Of Election Changes Instigated By Aggressive Members Who Want "In" And "Out" At Opportunistic Times Of Their Own Choosing.

Having applied for formal status as an LLC (as discussed in Chapters 2 and 3), your next concern is the type of entity classification you choose to be. You need to make said choice for Federal income tax purposes. When conducting any form of business for profit, sooner or later there will be an income tax return to be filed. It is better that you select the form of return, rather than letting the IRS select it for you. You have the option to do this via **Form 8832**: *Entity Classification Election.*

Before you can use Form 8832, however, you must have an entity name. This is that business name you used when you filed your LLC Articles of Organization with the Secretary of State for the state where your principal office will be. You also need an EIN: Employer Identification Number. Every business tax return that you file requires an EIN. The EIN is the **Tax ID** of the entity whether it is an employer or not. Where do you get an EIN?

From the IRS, of course. You may apply by phone, fax, online, or by mail. Whichever way, you need to have Form SS-4: *Application for Employer Identification Number*. This form not only identifies the principal owner of the business, but also its nature and type of activity, date business started, and number of employees expected (if any). Where do you get the EIN form? You may phone 1-800-829-3676 [1-800-TAX-FORM]. You'll get it much quicker if you go to the IRS's Internet website at **www.irs.gov**, click on Tax Forms, then download the form. While at it, also get Form 8832 and its instructions.

As a consequence of the above, our primary focus of this chapter is discussing and explaining Form 8832 to you. It is an important tax document. A copy is required to be attached to the return of each LLC member, the first taxable year in which the Form 8832 election is effective. The original of the form is filed with the IRS's Service Center in Philadelphia, PA (19255).

Because of new federal tax laws dealing with foreign trade, almost as much of Form 8832 is devoted to foreign LLCs as to domestic LLCs. As all national economies expand globally, some degree of engagement in foreign trade by small business is more a reality today than ever in the past. However, due to rules pertaining to "relevancy," U.S. "effectively connected" income, and the withholding of tax at source, we postpone any discussion on foreign LLCs until Chapter 8.

Apply for EIN First

Before filing Form 8832, you need to apply for an EIN: *Employer Identification Number*. As noted above, the EIN is a Tax ID of an *entity*, whether business or nonbusiness, or whether an employer or not. For this reason, we like to think of the "E" as for *Entity* rather than for "employer." Once assigned, the EIN dockets the entity from "day 1" until the entity no longer exists. The EIN is to an entity what the SSN (social security number) is to an individual person. It is a required Federal account number on all tax returns, information returns, and other communications with the IRS. One of the "other communications" is Form 8832 itself.

You need an EIN in order to process the entity classification election form. You can't get very tax far without it.

As also noted above, an EIN is assigned upon preparing and filing Form SS-4: *Application for Employer Identification Number*. This form consists of about 25 entry lines and about 35 checkboxes. At line 8a, for example, there are 15 checkboxes for indicating the type of entity you choose to be. The line 8a is officially captioned:

Type of entity (Check only one box). **Caution**: *If applicant is a limited liability company, see the instructions for line 8a.*

This is your first hint that there is an interaction between Form SS-4 and Form 8832 . . . or, vice versa. Hence, you need in hand both forms at the same time.

In relevant part, the instructions for line 8a say—

Check the box that best describes the type of entity applying for the EIN. **Caution:** *This is not an election for a tax classification of an entity. See "Limited Liability Company (LLC)" below.*

The instructions referred to "below" say—

• *If the entity is classified as a partnership for Federal tax purposes, check the "Partnership" box.* ☐*Partnership*

• *If the entity is classified as a corporation for Federal tax purposes, check the "Other corporation" box and write "LLC" in the space provided.* ☐*Other corporation* _____

• *If the entity is disregarded as an entity separate from its owner, check the "Other" box and write in "disregarded entity" in the space provided.* ☐*Other* _____

Thus, what the SS-4 instructions are saying is that, if you are an LLC, you have to decide what *tax classification* you want to be (corporation, partnership, or proprietorship) before completing line

8a. This is relatively easy to do. Because of the accounting and tax complications involved, most LLCs prefer not being taxed as a corporation. Only if you are a single-member LLC can you be taxed as a "disregarded entity." Otherwise, where there are two or more LLC members, a partnership entity is to be indicated. At this point on the SS-4, you are getting a foretaste of what Form 8832 is all about. There is an interaction . . . with a difference.

Other EIN Information

In other respects, Form SS-4 provides a good prognosis of what your "business model" ought to be. Various thought-provoking questions are asked. For example, you are asked—

- Reason for applying.
- Date business started or acquired.
- Closing month of accounting year.
- Principal business activity.
- Expected number of employees in the next 12 months.
- To whom most of the products or services are sold.

Other pertinent information is sought which necessitates that you read the five pages of instructions accompanying the SS-4. Said instructions are quite educational for synopsis-learning what is expected of you as a business owner, whether an LLC or other entity. Except for Federal taxation choice only, an LLC has to comply with all other tax laws that are currently in effect.

You should particularly read the SS-4 instructions at the section headed: *When to Apply for a New EIN*. Among other things, it tells you that if you become the owner of an existing business, do **not** use the EIN of the former owner. Get your own EIN. Otherwise, it would be like your using someone else's SSN on your tax return. The instruction also says: *File only one Form SS-4, regardless of the number of businesses operated or trade names used.* You are further told: *Do not apply for a new EIN if — you elected on Form 8832 to change the way the entity is taxed.*

Another "Do not apply for a new EIN" pertains to a partnership. In a partnership of any kind, members come and go. They sell, exchange, or gift their capital and profit interests (among friends, family, and associates) almost like that of stock in a corporation. When 50% or more of the total interests change hands in a 12-month period, the entity is allowed to make a short-year accounting so as to settle all old accounts. The following day, another short-year accounting resumes with new accounts, new capital, and new ownership percentages. The original EIN continues to be used, if the business operation itself has not materially changed.

Taking all of the above together, once an EIN is assigned to a partnership LLC, the same EIN can be used year in and year out, as members come and go. This is a tremendous symbolic convenience for the continuity of life of a successful LLC business. To discontinue an LLC, formal dissolution is required.

Purpose of Form 8832

Although cited earlier, we again cite the title of Form 8832. It is: *Entity Classification Election*. Keep the word "Election" foremost in mind. If you do not exercise your election rights in a timely manner (with Form 8832), you are automatically classified — for Federal tax purposes — under Default Rules. There are three basic default rules, namely:

A. Existing entity rule
B. Domestic entity rule
C. Foreign entity rule

An entity in existence before January 1, 1997 that has already established a Federal tax classification does not need to make an election to continue that classification. This applies to domestic and foreign entities alike. If an existing entity decides to change its tax classification, the use of Form 8832 is required.

The domestic default rules require that unless Form 8832 is used, the entity is either— (1) A partnership if it has two or more members, or (2) Disregarded as an entity if it has a single owner and, therefore, is taxed as a proprietorship. Comparable default rules apply to foreign unincorporated entities.

An election using Form 8832 directs how your LLC will be *income taxed* . . . for Federal tax purposes only. The election has no effect whatever on the limited liability features prescribed by state law. Most income taxing states, but not all, follow the Federal taxation election of Form 8832. Hence, the clear purpose of Form 8832 is to elect the taxing mode of an LLC. It does nothing more, and nothing less, than this.

The instructions to Form 8832 at: *Purpose of Form*, say—

For Federal tax purposes, certain business entities are automatically classified as corporations.

Automatic corporations are called *per se* (by means of itself) corporations. As such, they are organized under specific Federal or state law describing them as a corporation, incorporated, body corporate, body politic, joint-stock company, joint-stock association, insurance company, or banking institution.

Thus, all business entities that are not automatically per se corporations are "eligible entities" for purposes of Form 8832. The instructions then go on to say—

The IRS will use the information entered on this form to establish the entity's filing and reporting requirements for Federal tax purposes.

Information on the Form

If Form 8832 is an election-type form, we have to ask ourselves: "What information on the form makes it so special?" This is probably one of the simplest IRS forms that you'll ever see. In a condensed manner, we present its general contents to you in Figure 4.1. Note that it has eight distinctive stand-alone checkboxes. How much simpler can a tax form be than a series of straightforward checkboxes?

Also note that at the very first entry space, two items of information are required. These are: *Name of entity* and *EIN*. If you do not have an EIN, the instructions tell you to apply for one. We have already instructed you in this regard.

As you can see in Figure 4.1, there are six items of information required on the election form. The two most dominant items are: *Type of election* (2 checkboxes) and *Form of election* (6 checkboxes). Thus, there is a total of 8 checkboxes. The IRS refers to these as the: ***Check-the-box rules*** for (tax) ***Classification of Entities***.

ENTITY CLASSIFICATION ELECTION	FORM 8832

Name of Entity _____   EIN _____

1. Type of election

    a. ☐ Initial classification when newly formed

    b. ☐ Change in current classification

2. Form of entity

    a. ☐ Domestic association ... taxable as corporation

    b. ☐ Domestic entity ... taxable as partnership

    c. ☐ Domestic (single owner) ... taxable as proprietorship

    d. ☐ Foreign Association ... taxable as corporation

    e. ☐ Foreign entity ... taxable as partnership

    f. ☐ Foreign (single owner) ... taxable as proprietorship

3. Disregarded entity information

    a. Name of owner _____

    b. Tax ID of owner (SSN or EIN) _____

    c. Country of organization (if foreign) _____

4. Effective date of election _____ *m / d / yr* _____

5. Name of person for IRS contact _____

6. Phone number _____

Consent Statement & Signature(s)

Under penalties of perjury, I (we) _____

Signature(s)	Date	Title

Fig. 4.1 - Abbreviated Arrangement of Tax Classification Election Form

Item 3 addresses the single-member LLC — a disregarded entity — that is taxed as a proprietorship under federal law, and under state law (where income taxation is applicable). In addition, to maintain the LLC status, there is a state registration fee based on amount of income.

Items 4, 5, and 6 are self-explanatory. The month, day, and year (item 3) when the election is to go into effect starts the IRS's administrative and computer tracking programs for tax compliance. However, instructions say that the effective date can not be more than 75 days prior to the filing date, nor later than 12 months after the filing date. The "filing date" is the stamped date placed on the original of the form, when actually received by the IRS Center in Philadelphia, PA.

As to the two checkboxes at item 1 (Type of election), obviously only one box can be checked. Box 1a is for a newly-formed entity electing its initial classification. Box 1b is for an existing entity changing its current classification. The clear implication is that whatever your initial election was, you can change your tax classification at a later date. When you do this with box 1b, the coordination of the effective date with the accounting-period date of the former tax classification is crucial. You want to avoid any overlapping of the required tax reporting and filing requirements.

Checking "Form of Entity"

As self-evident in Figure 4.1, there are six checkboxes for electing one's *Form of entity* (at item 2). Obviously, only one box can be checked for each Form 8832 filed. If more than one box is checked inadvertently or intentionally, the election will be invalidated altogether. The entity default rules would then apply.

The wording at all six of the item 2 checkboxes contains a common phrase. That phrase is: *Eligible entity electing to be . . . .* Again, for emphasis, an "eligible entity" is *any* business arrangement that is **not** a per se (statutorily mandated) corporation. The importance of this concept is that Form 8832 is not the sole election province of LLC entities. In other words, a business arrangement does not have to be an LLC to be eligible to use Form 8832. Any unincorporated entrepreneur can use the form.

As to the six checkboxes on Form 8832, three are for domestic entities and three are for foreign entities. Whether domestic or foreign, the election is limited to being taxed as a corporation, a partnership, or a proprietorship. These are the three basic conventional business forms. There is no election option to be income taxed in any other way. There is no elective provision to be taxed as a trust (whether domestic or foreign), an exempt organization, a stock or commodity trader, a nonprofit corporation, an investment company, a personal holding company, or any other specially taxed entity.

When electing to be classified "as a corporation," the entity is automatically taxed as a C corporation. This means double income taxation, first at the entity level and again at the distributee level. If you want to avoid this double taxation — who doesn't? — you must attach to Form 8832 an S corporation election form. An S corporation is a pass-through entity similar in many accounting respects to a partnership. To make the S election, use Form 2553: *Election by a Small Business Corporation.* All we can do at this point is to alert you to the existence of Form 2553 if you prefer S-status to that of a C-status corporation. Often, an "association" of small capitalists in a common venture prefers not to register under state law as an LLC. In such cases, corporate status provides the accounting and managerial discipline necessary for entity success.

When not electing to be taxed as a corporation, and there are two or more contributing capitalists, the partnership form of Federal taxation is near optimal. We think partnership taxation is optimal for those who have already registered (à la Chapters 2 and 3) as an LLC. For others, the limited partnership form is preferable. In a limited partnership, the general partner can be a C corporation for limiting his personal liability in the joint venture. We'll devote an entire chapter to partnership taxation matters. We do so in Chapter 10: Partnership LLC Rules.

Where there is a single-member business endeavor, the proprietorship form is automatic. Unless the owner chooses to be an LLC, no Form 8832 is required. Without the form, the proprietor is solely and personally liable for his business decisions, and for those liability actions perceived to be associated with his business activities. To achieve some protection against personal liability, the proprietor may do one of three things, namely—

(i)   purchase a million-dollar liability insurance policy;
(ii) register as an LLC in his state of domicile; or
(iii) register as a C or S corporation (an unlikely preference where LLC is a choice).

If a single-member business registers as an LLC, he can elect on Form 8839 to be: *disregarded as a separate entity*. This frees him from the complexity of filing corporation tax returns, and enables him to continue filing Schedules C or F (Form 1040), as appropriate. As you'll learn in Chapter 5, single member LLCs require great attention to the tax and financial isolation of business affairs (for "entity shield" creation).

Consent Statement & Signature(s)

The entire lower one-third portion of Form 8832 is a signature block captioned: ***Consent Statement and Signature(s)***. The "consent statement" consists of an *Under penalties of perjury* statement that those who sign below consent to the tax classification election "indicated above." The statement goes on to establish that each signatory has examined the form and finds it to be "true, correct, and complete."

There are five signatory lines columned into *Signature, Date,* and *Title*. The instructions say that if more than five signatures are involved, a *Continuation Sheet* may be used. A continuation sheet can be another copy or two (or three) of blank forms, sequentially attached and numbered. Or, it can be a separate sheet of the entity's own making, exactly duplicating the consent statement and signature block format (highly abbreviated in Figure 4.1).

For a newly-formed LLC, the unanimous consent of all owner-members is required. Each member examines the election choice, signs and dates a signature line, then enters his/her/its "title." The common title for all signers would be: "LLC member." If there were 10 required signatures, for example, each signer could affix a sequential number, such as #1 of 10; #2 of 10; #3 of 10; . . . #10 of 10. This way all members can be fully accounted for in the consent statement and signature block of Form 8832.

When changing from one elected tax classification to another on Form 8832, only a majority of owner-member signatures is required. Better yet, if the Articles of Organization filed with state authorities so provide, an officer, manager, or designated member may sign for all members of the entity. A single signature is certainly a practical arrangement where members are scattered geographically throughout the U.S. and the world. But it carries some tax risk for the nonsigners. If operations turn sour in the business, or if rampant tax abuses are perceived, those who did not sign the consent statement have to swallow hard and pay their share of the consequences. Nonsigners of any document always have difficulty recalling why or what they did not sign. They will adamantly claim that the document was never fully explained.

The original Form 8832, when properly executed, is filed (as a separate document of its own) with the IRS Center at Philadelphia, PA 19255. One copy is attached to the entity's first tax return or other information return for the year in which the election is to take effect. A separate copy should be furnished to and retained by each owner-member of the LLC. We depict the importance of all of this in Figure 4.2.

The 60-Month Rule

There is a bit of wisdom in requiring all LLC owner-members to consent to the Form 8832 tax classification election. Presumably, each signer, protecting his own economic interests, acts as a check and balance on the other signers to see that business and tax affairs are conducted properly. In any venture, it takes a few operational years for matters to work themselves out and settle down into an objective business stride. This is the theory on which the 60-month rule is based.

Its substance is that once a tax election is made, the entity must endure 60 months (5 years) before changing to another tax classification. The exact official wording is prescribed in IRS Regulation § 301.7701-3(c)(1)(iv): *Elections; Limitation.* The pertinent wording is—

*If an eligible entity makes an election to change its classification . . . the entity cannot change its classification by election again during the **sixty** months succeeding the effective date of the election. . . . An election by a newly formed eligible* *entity that is effective on the date of formation is not considered a change for purposes* [hereof].

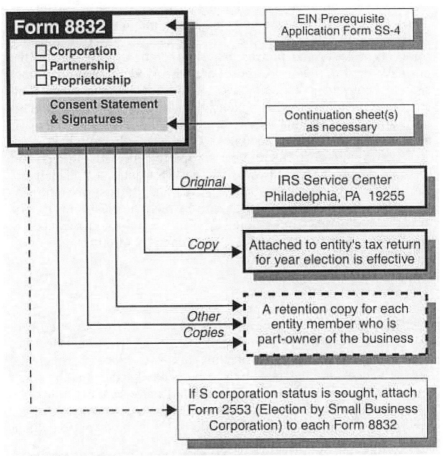

Fig. 4.2 - Notifying "Interested Parties" of Latest Income Tax Election

The idea is to avoid tax abuses by whipsaw. In any newly-formed business arrangement, members come and go. A change in membership alone is not a change in tax classification. Inevitably, though, there'll be one or more aggressive members who want to make their financial "kill" and get out. Before they get out, they persuade other members to change the tax classification to the aggressors' liking. Immediately after the effective date of change, the aggressors depart. This leaves the duped members to struggle with the tax accounting and debt reconciliation problems brought on by the change.

Because of infatuation with the "limited liability" concept of an LLC, our belief is that *tax whipsawing* and *debt whipsawing* could become widespread among LLC businesses. Somebody has to pay tax on the profits. Somebody has to satisfy suppliers, creditors, and customers. Somebody has to be responsible for clear-cut derelictions of duty. Being an LLC does not convey a "free pass" by any stretch.

Incidentally, the 60-month rule does not apply if an LLC is merged with or acquired by another business entity which has a different tax classification from that of the LLC's classification.

Furthermore, the IRS may permit a classification change within 60 months—

If more than 50% of the ownership interests in the entity, as of the effective date of the subsequent election, are owned by persons that did not own any interests in the entity on the filing date or on the effective date of the entity's prior election [as per Regulation citation above].

In way of summarizing the 60-month rule, we present Figure 4.3. The message intended there is that once an LLC is duly formed, it should stick to its initial classification until some truly bona fide business reason necessitates otherwise. This means giving the initial Form 8832 serious forethought and analysis.

Consequences of Change

There are four possible tax classification changes when using election Form 8832. The possibilities are:

1. A partnership elects to be an association, taxable as a corporation.
2. An association elects to be a partnership.
3. A solo corporation elects to be a disregarded entity, taxable as a proprietorship.
4. A disregarded entity elects to be an association, taxable as a solo corporation.

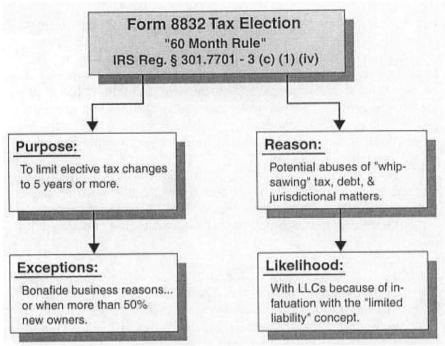

Form 8832 Tax Election
"60 Month Rule"
IRS Reg. § 301.7701 - 3 (c) (1) (iv)

Purpose:
To limit elective tax changes to 5 years or more.

Reason:
Potential abuses of "whip-sawing" tax, debt, & jurisdictional matters.

Exceptions:
Bonafide business reasons... or when more than 50% new owners.

Likelihood:
With LLCs because of in-fatuation with the "limited liability" concept.

Fig. 4.3 - Key Aspects of "60-Month Rule" on Tax Classification Changes

In no case, can a partnership (of two or more members) elect to be taxable as a disregarded entity (sole proprietorship). Conversely, in no case can a disregarded entity (single member) elect to be taxable as a partnership. The reason is obvious. Any two or more owners of a business must either be a partnership (by default) or an association (by election). Any single owner business must either be a proprietorship (by default) or a corporation (by election.)

When there are changes in membership of two or more, there is no change to the existing tax classification: partnership or association. When a two-member entity is reduced to one member, there is a default change to a disregarded entity (proprietorship). Conversely, when a single-member activity increases to two members, there is also a default change: to a partnership.

Whether a classification change is by election or by default, there are tax and accounting consequences. Form 8832 does nothing to change the relevant provisions of the Internal Revenue Code. There is a host of provisions applicable separately to corporations, partnerships, and proprietorships. Being an LLC does not change any of the established tax laws currently in effect. For example, when an LLC partnership changes to a corporation, it has to file a termination Form 1065 (as a partnership), then start its new classification under Form 1120 rules (as a C or S corporation). Or, if the LLC partnership is reduced to one member, it has to terminate the partnership, then start under Form 1040 rules: Schedule C (business) or Schedule F (farming).

In each case, membership capital accounting has to be closed on one date, then restarted the next day. The same applies to the earnings and profits of the entity. As long as the entity remains an LLC, no change in EIN is required. But if the entity reregisters under state law in a business form other than an LLC, a new EIN must be obtained. The more cavalier and undisciplined the business is run, the more complicated the change consequences become. The general effect of these consequences is depicted in Figure 4.4. After studying Figure 4.4, do you now see the wisdom of the 60-month rule?

Foreign Entity "Relevance"

One ordinarily thinks of a foreign entity as being owned by nonresident aliens, who seek to do business within the U.S. When said owners do so, they come under U.S. tax laws. Said tax laws apply only when *income* is derived by a branch of the foreign entity operating in the U.S. Such income is said to be "relevant" for U.S. tax withholding purposes.

The issue of relevancy of Form 8832 to foreign entities depends on what a withholding agent in the U.S. must do. Code Sections 1441 through 1446 cover the withholding of tax on U.S. income generated by nonresident aliens (as disregarded entities), foreign partnerships, and foreign corporations. Collectively, these sections are called: *collection-at-source* rules. That is, the U.S. tax (at "rounded rates") are collected and credited to a foreign entity's U.S. tax account, before money is transferred overseas to the entity owners. All collection-at-source rules are *very* complicated. Section 1441: ***Withholding of Tax on Nonresident Aliens***, for example, comprises over 1,200 statutory words and approximately 92,000 regulatory words! Relevant tax treaties, immigration rules, and international business arrangements complicate matters even further. U.S. classification is no longer relevant when a foreign entity ceases generating U.S. income for 60 consecutive months.

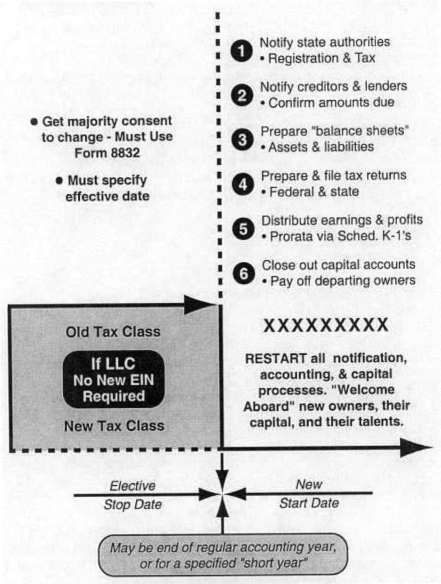

Fig. 4.4 - Paperwork Required When Changing Entity Tax Classification

5

SINGLE MEMBER LLCs

> As A "Disregarded Entity" Under Federal Law - A Proprietorship (One-Person) LLC - You Have To Document All Accounting Activities As Though You Were A Solo Corporation. This Means Preparing Schedule C (1040) With Particular Care In Separating Backup Schedules And Statements From Your Personal Activities. Anticipate Persistent Scrutiny Thereon. Claiming Office-In-Home (On Form 8829) Could Expose Your Personal Residence To Liability Attachment For Its Business-Use Portion. As A Surprise Defense, Disclose Your LLC Assets AND Business Liabilities On Schedule L (1040) "Balance Sheets."

Most states, not all, recognize single member LLCs. Those that do, include a statement in their *Formation Requirements* to the effect that—

*A limited liability company shall have **one** or more members.* [CCC Sec. 17050(b) where "CCC" is California Corporations Code. This is a restatement of Sec. 17001(t): *Definitions*, where a single member LLC is referred to as an "entity.]

Those states that do not recognize one-member LLCs legislate a comparable statement that—

*A limited liability company shall have **two** or more members.*

In all other respects, the formation requirements are identical. When the Articles of Organization are state-law officialized, a File Number is assigned and a checkbox is marked:

☒ *Single member LLC*

(Recall Figure 2.2 on page 2-10.)

As to any federal recognition, there is none! Form 8832: ***Entity Classification Election*** (in Chapter 4), with respect to ***Form of entity***, offers this checkbox:

☐ *A domestic eligible entity with a single owner electing to be disregarded as a separate entity.*

The effect of this IRS checkbox is that a single-owner LLC is a **proprietorship** under federal law.

Starkly stated, there is no federal tax form expressly titled: Limited Liability Company or Proprietorship LLC. Because of this reality, we need to explain how the LL (limited liability) shield is manifested with IRS tax forms for proprietorship filings. If you want the LLC benefits in a proprietorship, you must more stringently separate your business assets from personal assets than is customarily the practice for proprietorships. This means separation by **documentation**: not by oral intent. We'll tell you how to do this. Before doing so, however, we must inform you as to why the IRS treats a proprietorship LLC as a disregarded entity.

Why "Disregarded Entity" Status

The fundamental impetus for the creation of an LLC under state law is to circumvent the long-held legal thesis of *joint and several liability* of an unincorporated business. The term "joint and several" implies more than one member in the business arrangement. When more than one member joins in a venture to share in the earnings and profits, an accounting entity evolves. This entity is a necessity because of member differences in contributions of capital and property, differences in participative efforts, and differences in distributions of income or loss. Thus, due to the natural self-interests of the members themselves, an **entity** is formed.

An "entity" is a "thing" — a creation — separate and apart from the individual members in a joint venture. In the legal sense, an entity can sue, be sued, and make decisions on behalf of all members collectively. In an LLC arrangement, the entity can sue, and be sued, separately from its members. Any legal decision favoring the entity *adds* to its assets; any legal decision against the entity **subtracts** from its assets. It is better that entity assets be exposed than the personal assets of its owners.

In a proprietorship (single member) LLC, there is no formation of a natural entity. The owner and the business are one and the same. There is no natural separation for accounting and legal reasons. A separation can be made, but it is not a natural process of its own. The owner must work at it with books and records.

Enter now the IRS designation of a proprietorship LLC as a **Disregarded entity**. In the instructions to Form 8832, this designation is defined as—

A disregarded entity is an eligible entity that is treated as an entity that is not separate from its single owner. Its separate existence will be ignored for Federal tax purposes unless it elects corporate tax treatment.

In other words, a single member LLC has no liability shield protection, unless it elects to incorporate. To do so, it must apply for corporation status under the General Corporation Law of its home state. This is a whole different process from that in Chapter 2 for LLC formation.

It so happens that federal and state law both recognize a single-owner (called: solo) corporation. As mentioned earlier, all states do not recognize a solo LLC. This means that, if a sole proprietorship applies to become a corporation, there's no legal point in becoming an LLC. The corporate liability shield is much the same as an LLC liability shield.

We depict this aspect for you in Figure 5.1. There is one major practical difference, however. A sole LLC is much simpler — tax accounting and operationally — than a solo corporation. Thus, the key message that comes through is that a single member LLC must

ACT AS THOUGH it were a solo corporation. A proprietorship "acting like a corporation" is the thrust of that which follows.

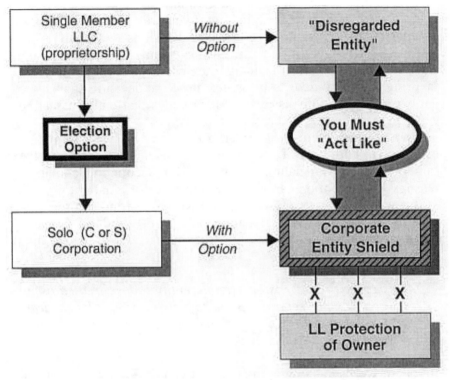

Fig. 5.1 - Resembling a Corporation in LLC Accounting

Initial Authenticating Papers

If you intend to do business as a single-member (proprietorship) LLC, there are two authenticating documents that you MUST HAVE at all times. Foremost is your *LLC Articles of Organization Certificate* authenticated by the Secretary of State for the state where your principal office is located. The second document is your *Fictitious Business Name Statement* authenticated by the Clerk-Recorder's office of the county (of the state) where you do business. For each of these documents you are assigned a File Number. The LLC file number remains the same so long as you do not change the entity form of business. The dba (**doing business as**) file number changes each time you renew your registration with the County Clerk-Recorder's office. It is not a bad idea to display on your proprietorship tax return your LLC #.

In Chapter 2, we covered the essentials of forming an LLC. We'll not repeat those procedures here. Whether a single-member or multi-member LLC, the application procedures and paperwork are the same. The only precaution to take is to make sure that your LLC entity name coincides with your county fictitious name. If you change your fictitious dba name, which you can do as often as you wish, you must also change it with the Secretary of State where your LLC # was issued. Each time you change your business name, a new dba File # is issued. However, you retain the same LLC #. There is a "filing fee" for all of this, of course.

In the case of your Fictitious Business Name Statement, **two** of your signatures are required. As a proprietorship, you sign on the left-hand side of the county registration form. As an LLC, you sign on the right-hand side of the same county form. As a proprietor, you are a ***Registrant***; as an LLC, you are an ***Officer of an Entity***.

The instructions for your officer signing say (depending on each county's registration form)—

If Registrant is a corporation, LLC, LLP, or LP, officer sign below [and complete the information requested]:

Entity name   (same as dba)
Officer signature   X (you sign)
Print name & title (print & add "Owner")
Certification # from Secretary of State (your LLC # & state)

This is all fine, until a lawsuit is filed against you. If you've been through a lawsuit before, you know the drill. The plaintiff's attorney will attack your business operation as a fraud. He will pull up your county dba statement on his computer and will print it out. He'll do the same for your LLC articles. Then he'll pick, pick away at every line on those documents, every entry on whatever line you made an entry, every checkbox you checked, and every signature you made. He'll do his darnedest to find a miniscule (and irrelevant) flaw and accuse you of willfully committing a crime. This tactic is perfectly legal in our system of justice.

Flaw Theory of Criminality

Here's an example of what we mean. On a fictitious business name statement form, there's a section of 12 checkboxes where you are directed to check **only one box** that—

This business is conducted by . . .

You checked: ☒ *husband & wife*. You could have checked the box captioned: ☐ *an individual* (for a proprietorship), or the box captioned: ☐ *limited liability company* (for an LLC). A husband and wife, by the way, are treated as one individual or as a one-member LLC. Nevertheless, the plaintiff's attorney is ecstatic. He's found the criminal flaw he needs to assault and embarrass you. He will bore in hard.

He drags you into court, calls you to the witness box, has the clerk administer the oath, shows you the dba document with your signature, then submits the document into evidence. He points to your signature on the left-hand side, then asks you to read the preprinted Registrant statement above your signature. It reads—

I declare that all information in this statement is true and correct. (A registrant who declares as true information which he or she knows to be false is guilty of a crime.)

"That's it, Your Honor. He's guilty of a crime! The liability protection he asserts does not exist. Your Honor, I move that the Court order the defendant's LLC status be null and void, and that my client be paid $1,000,000 (1 million) for damages."

"Objection!" your attorney jumps up and says. "My client checked the box ☒ *husband & wife* because they both indeed conduct the business. Besides, the LLC status is clearly disclosed on the right-hand side of the dba document by setting forth the entity name, officer signature, and File # of the Secretary of State's Certification (as an LLC)."

The Judge responds: "Objection granted; let's move on."

Are you beginning to get our point? Lawsuits can be cruel, inhumane, and lacking in common sense.

The adding of the letters LLC to your business name will not deter a disgruntled customer from suing for some perceived misdeed, defect, or irregularity of your business activities. You've got to dot every "i" and cross every "t" in your liability shield documentation. You start off right when preparing your proprietorship tax return. When a lawsuit comes, every accounting document you have prepared will be subpoenaed and compared with that of a full blown corporation.

Head Portion of Schedule C (1040)

In the federal domain, there are two basic tax forms for a proprietorship. One is Schedule C (Form 1040); the other is Schedule F (Form 1040). The Schedule C is titled: *Profit or Loss from Business (Sole Proprietorship)*. The Schedule F is titled: *Profit or Loss from Farming*. The accounting for income and expenses on these two tax schedules is functionally comparable. For most of our readers, however, Schedule C (Form 1040) is probably more LLC instructive.

Form 1040, as you know, is titled: *U.S. Individual Income Tax Return*. Heed now your reality precaution. Since your Schedule C business tax form attaches directly to your individual (personal) tax return, your LL shield, per se, is nonexistent. You have to establish that such a shield does indeed exist. Let's start doing this on the head portion of your Schedule C.

The head portion of Schedule C (1040), abbreviated as necessary, is presented in Figure 5.2. Particularly note that there are eight alphabetized lines of entry spaces A through H. The line spaces for entering the true name of the proprietor and his social security number are unalphabetized. This is simply for consistent identity purposes when being attached to Form 1040. Your personal name has no immediate liability attack significance. Better to concentrate on lines A, B, C, and D.

Line A asks for a short description of your principal business activity. To exemplify, suppose it is: *Sales and service of bicycles (nonmotor driven)*. This description is all you need. It gives the IRS a good idea how most — meaning 90% or so — of your business income is derived. But, if the other 10% is derived from the sales and service of firearms (hand guns, shoulder rifles, etc.)

and one of your customers accidentally injures a friend, can't you see how liability vulnerable you are?

Schedule C (Form 1040)	Profit or Loss From Business	Tax Year
Name of proprietor		SSN
A Principal business		B Activity code
C Business name		D EIN
E Business address		
F Accounting method: ☐ cash ☐ accrual ☐ other		
G Did you "materially participate"? ☐ yes ☐ no		
H Check if business started this year ▶ ☐		

● Gross receipts or sales	● Cost of goods sold
● Operating expenses	● Miscellaneous expenses
● Depreciation Form 4562	● Office-in-home Form 8829

Fig. 5.2 - The Head Portion of Schedule C (1040) & Other

Line B asks that you select a 6-digit IRS-designated business activity code from a list of **318** "industry codes" for proprietorships. The selection instructions say—

Select the category . . . and activity that best identifies the principal source of your sales or receipts.

For sales and service of bicycles, the designated code would be: **451110** (for sporting goods). For that 10% sales and service of firearms, the activity code would be: **114210** (hunting & trapping). To the IRS, code 45110 would be highly acceptable. To an angry liability litigant, your omitting of code 114210 could be construed as a major criminal flaw against you.

Line C asks for your *Business name.* Be sure that you use your **entity** name: the same one that you used when filing your fictitious business name statement with your county clerk's office, **and** that which you used when filing for LLC status with your Secretary of State. For our example situation above, your entity name could be:

A-1 Mountain Bikes, LLC #_____

Though it is not often done, we suggest (for Schedule C purposes only) that you include your state's LLC File #. Doing so adds a tone of authenticity to your one-member LLC and "teases" a potential adversary to go check it out for himself (via the Secretary of State's web page).

Line D asks for your *Employer* ID # (EIN). We want to stress that it is an **Entity** EIN whether you have employees or not. To apply for an EIN (if you don't already have one), use IRS Form SS-4: *Application for* . . . . Be sure to enter your entity name at line 1, and of the 16 checkboxes for *Type of Entity*, you check the box ☒ *Other (specify)* ▶ _____. Then enter in the blank space provided: *LLC, single member.*

By means of Lines A, B, C, and D on Schedule C (1040), your goal is to convince would-be litigants of your LLC consistency. You want to do this particularly with respect to your: (1) Entity name, (2) Entity EIN, and (3) Entity LLC File #. You want to do so in a way that overwhelms the *Disregarded entity* status that IRS Form 8832 (in Chapter 4) pins on you.

Likely Flaw Targets: Income

Schedule C (1040) is one of several income accounting schedules that attach to your federal Form 1040. Except for Schedule F (for farming), it is the only schedule where your LLC status is proclaimed. If a liability lawsuit is filed against you and you want to claim the LLC protection, your entire Schedule C — with all attachments — is fair legal game. If you cannot survive the flaw scrutinizing process, your personal assets are at risk.

With this prelude, we present in Figure 5.3 a diagrammatic overview of Schedule C with its attachments and backups. Potentially, some or all could be subpoenaed in court. For the official version of any of the tax forms identified, we urge that you visit the IRS's website: **www.irs.gov** and check on Tax Forms. Otherwise, keep in mind that a legal adversary would be rummaging for whatever liquid assets and quick sale marketables your LLC entity owns. The adversarial stance will be that you have placed those assets beyond reach of the court.

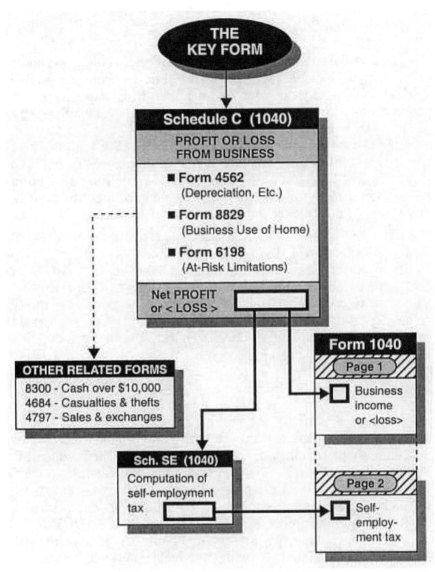

Fig. 5.3 - Tax Forms Associated with a Proprietorship

Foremost in this regard is Line 1 on your Schedule C: *Gross receipts or sales.* You know, or should know, that, as a liability defendant, your Line 1 dollars-in will be probed ad infinitum. For this, your income ledger (daily, weekly, monthly), your LLC bank account, your invoicing procedures, letterhead correspondence, and other related dollar-denominated documents will be ruthlessly screened. Basically, the plaintiff wants to know the total amount of money taken in, how that money was handled, and what's the balance in your bank account. Make sure that your LLC bank account is consistent with your entity name on Schedule C and your entity EIN.

Also, in the income category, there's an end-of-year inventory in your *Cost of goods sold*. Said inventory, if of consequence, is a marketable asset. How you determined this inventory could play a major role in the credibility of your accounting records. Any slipshodness that comes through will be interpreted as a willful attempt to defraud the plaintiff.

On all profit or loss business tax returns, there is one final income item called: *Other income (explain)*. If this amount is more than $1,000 you'd better have each source and amount documented and well substantiated. Plaintiff's attorneys often act like IRS tax auditors; they try to embarrass and fluster you. They want to back you into a corner and force you to admit that you have some unreported income. If your total other reported income is less than $1,000 and the plaintiff persists in harassing you, you know he has a weak case.

Expense-Side Flaw Targets

There are about 25 tax allowable expense categories on Schedule C (1040), as per Figure 5.4. No plaintiff's attorney is going to query you on each and every category. That's the IRS's audit job. But he will pick, snarl, and chew over selected categories that are most likely to produce flaws of misrepresentation and fraudulent practices on your part. Count on every inconsistency being blown out of proportion to reality. The process is a display of lawyer egotism and arrogance. We exemplify with five potential targets, namely:

(1) Advertising,
(2) Depreciation,
(3) Insurance,
(4) Legal services, and
(5) Meals & entertainment

Schedule C : Expense Categories			
Sequence	ITEM		Amount
001	Advertising	(printing & promotions)	
002	Bad debts	(accrual method only)	
003	Bank charges	(include credit cards)	
004	Car & truck expenses	(business only)	
005	Commissions	(paid to others)	
006	Contract labor	(nonemployees)	
007	Depreciation	(from Form 4562)	
008	Dues & pubs.	(seminars & newsletters)	
009	Employee benefits	(food, prizes, & awards)	
010	Freight out	(postage & parcel post)	
011	Insurance	(business only)	
012	Interest: Mortgage	(on business realty)	
013	Interest: Other	(on business loans)	
014	Laundry & cleaning	(include uniforms)	
015	Legal & professional	(consultants)	
016	Office expense	(stationery & other)	
017	Pension plans	(for employees only)	
018	Rent	(paid on business property)	
019	Repairs	(painting & maintenance)	
020	Supplies	(small tools & materials)	
021	Taxes	(payroll, property, licenses)	
022	Travel & lodging	(documented)	
023	Meals & entertainment	(less 20% for yourself)	
024	Phone & utilities	(business only)	
025	Wages	(gross amount: nonshop)	
026 to 030	Other expenses	(SPECIFY)	

Fig. 5.4 - Preprinted Expense Lines on Schedule C (1040)

As to advertising expenditures, your adversary will want to see your print ads, Internet ads, and other written or oral statements of promises you made . . . and didn't keep. And, of course, he'd want to see any complaints on file concerning products sold or services rendered by your organization.

As to depreciation allowances, your adversary will have been coached by his tax professional enough to quiz you on Forms 4562 and 4562W. Form 4562 is titled: *Depreciation and Amortization*, and Form 4562W is the *Worksheet* therewith. Form 4562 lists all business property acquisitions in the current year. Form 4562W tabulates all property acquired and placed in service in prior years, and still in use in the current year. You can expect to be asked to supply a detailed market valuation of all machinery, equipment, tools, vehicles, structures, and real estate used in your LLC business. If you don't supply, you can be court ordered to do so, or face monetary penalties for contempt. Furthermore, you are likely to be court instructed not to dispose of any of your Form 4562 items until the liability complaint is resolved.

As to insurance expenditures, be sure to dig up and have available for adversarial inspection all liability-type policies. This would include errors and omissions, accident coverage, produce and service warranties, etc. Have at least one blanket insurance policy to cover ordinary complaint-type risks in your line of business. Having such indicates that you are exercising reasonable care and prudence in providing for ordinary liability risks. Otherwise, you'll be hammered for willful neglect: a flaw that can be used to disregard your LL shield protection.

As for legal expenditures, if any, you'll be asked if you've been sued before. You may counter query as to what is meant by the term "before." The adversary's hostile response will be: "At *any time* in the past, whether business or personal!" Now you have to confess to that $732.63 Small Claims Court case that you lost some six years or so ago. This is another one of those pesky flaws that will be ballooned way out of proportion to the liability complaint that may be at hand.

As for meals and entertainment — a tough sell to the IRS — they can be a fertile source of tormentive inquiry. The target would be whom you wined and dined with respect to problems and complaints. What was the nature of the complaints, etc. etc.? Deal with this the best you can. The questions are only meant to expose your free-wheeling business style. Your LL shield provides no likely protection to this kind of rummaging.

Office-in-Home Surprise

Many proprietorships (whether LLC or not) conduct business out of their personal homes. For certain activities, doing so is a convenient and economical way to keep the business going during slow periods. The IRS recognizes the legitimacy of this practice by adopting a special tax form for it. Such is Form 8829: *Expenses for Business Use of Your Home* ▶ *File only with Schedule C (1040)*. This is the consequence of IRC Section 180A(c) which requires that the designated portion of one's dwelling be used *regularly and exclusively* as your principal place of business. If so used, that portion converts to business property.

Form 8819 expands on the above statutory recognition. Its very first three lines are—

1. Area used for business purposes   _____ sq.ft.
2. Total area of home   _____ sq.ft.
3. Business use percentage (divide 1 by 2) _____ %

When defensively claiming LLC status as your LL shield, can't you sense how a plaintiff's attorney is going to grill you endlessly about lines 1 and 2 on Form 8829? He's going to ask in great detail how you determined the square footages on those lines. He'll stop at nothing less than a careful diagram showing the measured spaces of your office and home. Something along the lines of Figure 5.5 would be required.

Using the dimensions in Figure 5.5 for illustration purposes, your business use of home space would be:

$$365 \text{ sq. ft} \div 2{,}170 \text{ sq. ft.} = 16.82\%$$

What comes next — on the witness stand in court — should not surprise you. "What is your home presently worth?," counsel will ask. You'd better have some documented answer, or the court will order that a professional appraisal be obtained. On the advice of your own attorney, suppose you had a statement that it was worth $594,530. The corresponding business portion market value would be:

$$\$594{,}530 \times 16.82\% = \$100{,}000$$

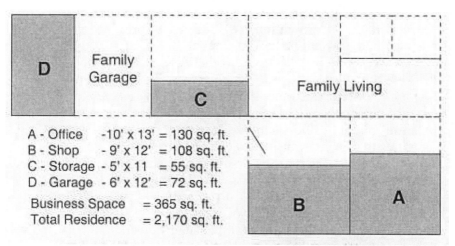

Fig. 5.5 - Measurement of Space: Business Use of Home

"Aha!" says the plaintiff's counsel. "You've just admitted that you have an LLC asset, readily marketable, that's worth $100,000. Since you claimed a business use deduction for it, it is **not** your personal property. It is your LLC business property, which we can — and will — go after."

He then turns to the Judge and says: "Your Honor, I move for a judgment lien against Mr. LLC's personal residence in the amount of $100,000 . . . or at least a stay order prohibiting his home from being sold until this matter is resolved."

Are you getting our point!

Just don't be too cocky in a vigorous defense of your LLC status. Don't cash starve your business on the premise that, when the legal chips fly, your business entity has no assets that can be attached. Anticipate some surprise. If you can't do so, we have one for you.

The Coup de Grâce

Earlier in this chapter, we pointed out that for federal purposes a single-member LLC is a *disregarded entity*. To establish your LLC credentials, you must do so under state law. Or, you could elect to be a one-person corporation. If no such election is made, then you have to "act like" a corporation. This means keeping all LLC entity assets separate and distinct from your personal assets.

To act like a corporation, what single form of accounting documentation would be best to pursue?

Answer: ***Balance Sheets*** . . . otherwise tax known as *Schedule L.* Note the plural "sheets." There are two balance sheets: one at *Beginning of year,* the other at *End of year.* In between the two are changes during the year. Each sheet is a listing of all assets and all liabilities of the business entity. The difference between assets and liabilities is your net worth, also called: *Owner's capital.*

Ordinarily, a sole proprietorship is not required to provide a set of balance sheets. But, as an LLC, the only convincing way to support your entity status is to prepare a full and accurate accounting of assets and also of liabilities. Instead of using the corporate Schedule L as a model, we suggest using the partnership Schedule L. This is because a multi-member LLC is a partnership for which a Schedule L is required. As slightly modified, our version of a one-owner Schedule L is presented in Figure 5.6. Be sure to prepare a Schedule L — which we designate as Schedule L (1040) — for each year you claim LL protection.

If you do so, when a cocky plaintiff's attorney crescendos towards his coup de grâce against you, you are prepared for this question and its insinuations:

"Mr. LLC, you allege that you are an entity with assets separate and apart from your personal assets. Is this correct?"

Your answer: "Yes, that's correct."

"Well, Mr. LLC, do you maintain any balance sheet type of accounting of your total assets and total liabilities . . . any at all? If so, does it show your net worth?"

Your answer: "Yes, here are my Schedules L (1040) for the past three years. I also have them as far back as year 2000 when I started my one-person LLC business. Do you want to see all of them . . . or just the most recent one?"

Rarely would a plaintiff's attorney answer you directly. He'll just move on to outlining his client's alleged damages against you, and to probing the value of your "quick sale" assets.

Schedule L (Form 1040)	BALANCE SHEETS				Tax Year	
Assets		**Start of Year**		**End of year**		
1	Cash					
2	Accounts receivable					
	• less bad debts	<	>		<	>	
3	Investments (specify)					
4	Loans receivable					
5	Depreciable assets					
	• less cumulative	<	>		<	>	
6	Amortizable assets					
	• less cumulative	<	>		<	>	
7	Depletable assets					
	• less cumulative	<	>		<	>	
8	Land					
9	Other (specify)					
	Total Assets					
Liabilities & Capital		**Start of Year**		**End of year**		
1	Accounts payable					
2	Loan payable < 1 yr					
3	Other liabilities < 1 yr					
4	Nonrecourse loans					
5	Loans payable > 1 yr					
6	Other liabilities > 1 yr					
	Total Liabilities					
7	Owner's capital					
Total Liabilities & Capital						

Ed. Note: (1) Total liabilities & capital equals total assets.
(2) Assets less liabilities = net worth = owner's capital

Fig. 5.6 - Projected Version of Schedule L (1040) for One-Owner LLCs

Your LLC status under state law is not an escape from those liabilities incurred in the ordinary course of business. By preparing a Schedule L (1040), you acknowledge your customary liabilities, as you should.

Expect More Badgering

Exhibiting in court an unofficial Schedule L (Form 1040) is like taunting a lion with red meat. With trained ferocity, the plaintiff's attorney will badger you on and on. The liabilities that you summarized on Schedule L — accounts payable, loans payable, other payables — will be torn apart and sniffed at. The sniffing will attempt to establish that you assumed the liabilities **after** the date on which you were served an *Endorsed-Filed* copy of the lawsuit against you.

For example, suppose that legal service was made upon you on May 2nd. The service was accompanied by an ORDER to appear in court on September 15th. On May 24th, you borrowed $100,000 from your bank to acquire much-needed equipment and inventory for your business. The tone of inquiry will be hostile and sneering. You'll be accused of taking on this added liability intentionally to deprive the plaintiff of his rightful due. You have to convince the court that, for pure business reasons, you could not wait until after the lawsuit was settled to make the purchases that you did.

If you survive the scorching scrutiny, you'll be asked to verify your *Owner's capital* at the last entry line in Figure 5.6. You'll be forced to testify that, if the court's decision went against you, the amount so entered would be immediately available for payover to the plaintiff. If you can do this, and the accuracy of your accounting is otherwise beyond reproach, this is the extent of your liability under LLC law. At this point, the gavel comes down: *Court adjourned!*

6

MULTI-MEMBER LLCs

Federal Taxation Rules Treat A Multi-Member LLC As A Partnership. A Special Checkbox On Form 1065 Provides For This. Once Checked, The Term "Partner" Is Construed To Mean "LLC Member." An LLC, In And Of Itself, Is NOT A Taxable Entity. Instead, All Net Income, Net Loss, Credits, And Certain Deductions "Pass Through" - Via Schedules K And K-1 - To Individual Members For Inclusion On Their Forms 1040. The Hallmark For Limited Liability Protection Is Schedule L: A Balance Sheet Of Assets, Liabilities, And Capital. If No Schedule L, The Credibility Of The LLC Is Open To Legal Attack.

Technically, any two or more members — be they persons or entities — can become a multi-member LLC. There is a subtechnicality, however, that should be considered. In a two-member LLC, should one become dissatisfied or become unable to continue with the arrangement (for whatever reason), the two-member entity has automatically self-converted (defaulted) to a single member LLC. This means that all two-member operating agreements are canceled and all two-member entity accountings and tax reportings are discontinued.

If each of the two former members wishes to continue in business on his or her own, then a situation develops where there is one of the following: (1) a single member LLC and a sole proprietor; (2) two sole proprietors; or (3) two single member LLCs. In any case, the self-conversion triggers a great amount of additional work for recertification, renaming, re-EINing, reprogramming books of account, and notifying the IRS of changes in tax filing status. It is better, we think, that a two-member LLC **not get started** than to risk the default conversion into two proprietorship-type activities.

It is much better, we think, to start with a *three* (or more) member LLC. This way, should one member bail out or become deceased, the remaining two members (or more) can persuade other persons or entities to fill the void. The desired result is the continuity of effort to make the LLC succeed in the chosen principal business endeavor.

Once you start with three or more members, and you immediately replace those who bail out, you have a good old-fashioned partnership form of enterprise on your hands. We want to tell you about the tax and operating arrangements involved, and how they differ so much from a single member LLC.

Partnership Return: Form 1065

The IRS publishes over **1,500** — yes, one thousand, five hundred (1,540 by our count) — tax forms and schedules. If you scan the topical Index to these forms, you will not find among the "L"s a form captioned: *Limited Liability Company.* Nor will you find such a form on the IRS's website: **www.irs.gov**. Search and click on all you want, you'll find no Form wxyz: Limited Liability Company. You have to know, be told, or take our word for it that the applicable form is that of a partnership. Said item is Form 1065: *U.S. Return of Partnership Income.* You can find this form on the IRS's website, and we urge that you do. Print out pages 1 and 2 thereof. Scan through page 1, and see if you can find the term "limited liability company" thereon. Page 1 consists of a head portion, an income portion, a deductions portion, and a signature block. As with all U.S. tax forms, the signature block starts off with a jurat clause: *Under penalties of perjury,* etc.

In the signature block, in small print words below the signature line, you'll find—

Signature of general partner or limited liability company member manager.

This instruction tells you that, if your entity is a partnership, the general partner must sign. If an LLC, the member-manager must sign. The signature space accommodates one or the other, not both. This is your first positive tip-off that an LLC (multi-member) must use **Form 1065**.

Page 2 of Form 1065 consists of Schedule A: *Cost of Goods sold*, Schedule B: *Other Information*, and a space labeled: ***Designation of Tax Matters Partner*** (TMP). The instructions tell you that a TMP must be a general partner and that for an LLC . . .

Only a member-manager of the LLC is treated as a general partner. A member-manager is any owner of an interest in the LLC who, alone or together with others, has the continuing exclusive authority to make the management decisions necessary to conduct the business for which the LLC was formed [in the state where registered].

The TMP does not sign the return. He/she is a designee (one designated) by name, address, and Tax ID.

As to Schedule B: Other Information, item 1 asks:

1. *What type of entity is filing this return?   Check applicable box* [not more than one]:

a ☐ *Domestic general partnership*

b ☐ *Domestic limited partnership*

c ☒ *Domestic limited liability company*

d ☐ *Domestic limited liability partnership*

e ☐ *Foreign partnership*

f ☐ *Other* ▶ ....

Check box **c** (as we've done above) and — presto — your Form 1065 is converted into the equivalent: ***U.S. Return of LLC Income***. Thereafter, whenever you see the word "partner" or "partnership" on Form 1065, you substitute the equivalent word: "member" or "LLC". This may require mental gymnastics to keep all matters straight and could cause some awkward ambiguities. Our view is that, with the increasing popularity of LLCs, there could evolve a Form 1065 LLC.

Headview: LLC Form 1065

To see how the substitution of terminology works, let's look at the head portion of Form 1065. There's a bold outlined box at its very top. Below the substituted title: **U.S. Return of (Partnership) LLC Income**, entries call for the name and address of the filing entity. As a multi-member LLC, you would enter the registered name filed with the Secretary of State in your home state. Use the full correct name followed by the letters "LLC". This is important because the preprinted form uses the term "partnership" whereas you want to go on record immediately as being an LLC.

At this point, we lay out the head portion of Form 1065 in Figure 6.1. For space reasons, we abbreviate the official wording. We particularly want to call to your attention the nine bold-alphabetized items: **A** through **I**.

Form 1065	U.S. Return of LLC Income		Tax Year
A.	Name of LLC	D.	
B.	Street, Suite, P.O. Box	E.	
C.	City, State, ZIP	F.	
G.	Check applicable boxes: ☐ ☐ ☐ ☐ ☐		
H.	Check accounting method: ☐ ☐ ☐ _____		
I.	Number of **Schedules K-1** (one for each LLC member) ▶ _____		

Fig. 6.1 - Head Portion of LLC-Adapted Form 1065

The official wording of items A through E is:

A. Principal business activity _____
B. Principal product or service _____
C. Business code number _____
D. Employer identification number _____
E. Date business started _____

The one term that comes through most is the word: *business*. This implies that the multi-member LLC must be some legal trade or business which is not a tax shelter, or a financial scam, or a special family trust (whether domestic or foreign). We feel compelled to point this out because some states (California, for example: § 17002) legislate that an LLC

may engage in any lawful business activity, **whether or not for profit** . . . [Emphasis added.]

This emphasized clause, we submit, is an invitation to abusive practices that we see forthcoming in cash starved LLCs.

Item **F**: *Total assets*, requires showing the dollar amount entry from Schedule L: **Balance Sheets**, at the end of the tax year. Instructions for this item say that no entry is required if the total assets are less then $600,000. Can't you sense the LLC membership infighting to keep item F blank? When a liability lawsuit is filed, the first adversarial target is the total assets information. If there is no entry at item F, the arrangement will be ridiculed as a sham. Whereupon, the liability protection of the balance sheets and other accounting practices will be ignored.

Items **G** and **H** (in Figure 6.1) are checkboxes. They are quite self-explanatory on the official version of Form 1065. **G** is for type of return; **H** is for accounting method.

Item **I** requires entering the number of Schedules K-1 that are attached. The preprinted instructions at this item (with the word "partner" substituted with "member") read—

Attach one [Schedule K-1] *for each person who was a member* [of the LLC] *at any time during the tax year.*

If you are not already familiar with a K-1, just be aware that this is a tax information pass-through document. Because a K-1 entity pays no direct tax itself, all tax and financial matters pass through prorata to each member. Thereafter, each member prepares his/her/its own income tax returns. The most common of such returns are:

Form 1040 — U.S. Individual *Income Tax* Return
Form 1041 — U.S. *Income Tax* Return for Estates and Trusts [after death of an individual]
Form 1120 — U.S. Corporation *Income Tax* Return

Be aware that the term "Income Tax" does **not** appear in the preprinted title to Form 1065!

Where on Form 1040?

It would be helpful if you had a Form 1040 in front of you. Look for the *Income* portion on its page 1. There are 15 lines there for entering different types of income or loss. Do you see any line caption with the term: Limited liability company or LLC? As a person interested in LLC affairs, wouldn't you expect to find some line on Form 1040 for reporting LLC income or loss? It's there indirectly . . . but you have to know where to look.

We informed you above that multi-member LLC matters are reported to the IRS on Form 1065 (for partnerships). Where on Form 1040 is there any mention of partnerships? It's there on **line 17** (year 2005 version). Said line reads—

Rental real estate, royalties, partnerships, S corporations, trusts, etc. ***Attach Schedule E.***

Schedule E (Form 1040) is titled: ***Supplemental Income and Loss***. In short, Schedule E is for the reporting of income and loss from passive activities (rental real estate and royalties) and from participation in pass-through entities (partnerships, LLCs, S corporations, and trusts). Schedule E consists of five parts, of which only Part II is of LLC interest herein. Part II of Schedule E is titled: ***Income or Loss from Partnerships and S Corporations***. We believe that within a few years this title will be enhanced to include LLCs. In the meantime, you have to mentally associate your LLC activities with partnership activities.

Part II is at the top of page 2 of Schedule E (Form 1040). Where and what do you have to report? To aid you in this regard, we present in Figure 6.2 highlights of the candidate applicable items that address an LLC. We have indicated a bottom line there, which is not the bottom line of the entire Schedule E form. We are assuming that your only supplemental activity is an LLC. On this basis, you can see that the bottom line of Part II is a combination of information from checkboxes, columns, line entries, and other separate forms that you may have to attach to your Form 1040.

Part II Sch.E (1040)	Income or Loss From Partnerships, S Corporations, [and LLCs]			Year	
If at-risk activity : Form 6198				At Risk?	
Name of Entity		Type	Tax I.D.	All	Some
A					
B					
C					

PASSIVE Income/Loss		NONPASSIVE Income/Loss			
Loss From Form 8582	Income From Schedule K-1	Loss From Schedule K-1	Sec. 179 Exp. Form 4562	Income From Schedule K-1	
A					
B					
C					

	Add all income amounts		
	Add all loss & Sec. 179 amounts	< >	
	● Combine & enter result on page 1, Form 1040		

Fig. 6.2 - Part II, Sch. E (Form 1040) **Abbreviated for Instructional Purposes**

Note in Figure 6.2 that there are three forms, one section, and one schedule mentioned. We have indicated these in bold print. While not indicated on the official Part II, the titles of these particular items are:

Sec. 179 — Election to Expense Certain Depreciable Business Assets
Form 4562 — Depreciation and Amortization
Form 6198 — At-Risk Limitations
Form 8582 — Passive Activity Loss Limitations
Schedule K-1 — Partner's Share of Income, Deductions, Credits, etc. [Read "Partner's" as "LLC Member's" share . . .]

Also note in Figure 6.2 that there are two major columnar spacings. One column (consisting of two subcolumns) is captioned: *Passive Income and Loss*. The other column (consisting of three subcolumns) is captioned: *Nonpassive Income and Loss.* Do you know the difference? Your LLC may have elements of both. (Read *passive* as: general oversight of rental income activity; read *nonpassive* as: material, hands-on participation in the principal business of the LLC.) Do you know what Forms 4562, 6198, and 8582 are about? Your LLC reportings may involve any one or all three of these forms.

Additionally, not includible in Figure 6.2 is investment income and loss derived from stocks, bonds, mutual funds, and other assets. For LLC purposes, capital invested elsewhere than in the entity activity (or activities) is regarded as a tertiary level of endeavor. An LLC is not intended to be a personal holding company taxable as a publicly-traded corporation.

Our message is: There is no quick-fix, one figure, bottom-line amount that you can pluck out of the LLC air and enter it on Form 1040 as your share of an LLC's net income or net loss.

With the exception of Schedule K-1 (Form 1065), most of the other terms and forms that we show in Figure 6.2 are covered, or at least mentioned in subsequent chapters.

Overview of Schedule K-1

As previously indicated, the LLC-revised title of Schedule K-1 (Form 1065) is: *Member's* [Singular] *Share of Income, Deductions, Credits, etc*. This is a 2-page form: front and back. The front page consists of two columns: left and right. The left-hand column consists of information on the LLC and on the participating LLC member. The right-hand column consists of some 40+ spaces for the entry of pass-through dollar amounts. The back page consists of a listing of slightly over 100 instructional directions for transferring the front page information and dollar amounts onto each member's own income tax return. In addition, Schedule K-1 is accompanied by 12 pages of 3-columnar instructional text comprising about 8,600 words!

There is far more to Schedule K-1 than we can address at this point. For this reason, we urge that, as an LLC member, you procure a complete copy (with instructions) from the IRS by phone, or from its website [**www.irs.com**]. In the meantime, we present its general format in Figure 6.3. We want to highlight for you a few points that the official instructions tend to gloss over.

Sched. K-1	Form 1065	Year	Income <loss> items	15 lines
Member's Share of Income, Deductions, Credits, etc.				
I ▨ **Info About the LLC** ▨			Deductions	4 lines
Tax I.D. (EIN) Name, address IRS Center where filed Tax Shelter? ☐ ☐ ☐			Credits	2 lines
II ▨ **Info About the Member** ▨			Self-employment	2 lines
Tax I.D. (SSN or EIN) Name, address Type of member: ☐ ☐ ☐ ☐			Foreign transactions	7 lines
L. Member's share of capital Beginning % Ending %			AMT items	3 lines
M. Member's share of liabilities • Nonrecourse $ • Qualified $ • Recourse $			Tax-exempt income	3 lines
			Distributions	2 lines
N. Member's capital account • Beginning $ • Contributed $ • Current Year Change $ • Withdrawals $ • Ending $ ☐ ☐ ☐ ☐			Other information	4 lines
			IV ▨ **For IRS Use Only**	

Fig. 6.3 - General Format of Schedule K-1 (Form 1065)

In Part I of Figure 6.3, there are three checkboxes. They relate mostly to tax shelter activities and abuses therewith. More and more, the IRS is homing in on abusive practices of pass-through entities. In the past, the principal focus of attention has been on partnerships, S corporations, and trusts. Because so, these days there has been an explosion in multi-member LLC formations. This is caused by the giddy fascination in the belief that the letters "LL" place all members above the reach of tax and legal authorities. So, be on the alert for the IRS to target your LLC as a tax shelter or as some other abusive arrangement.

In Part II of Figure 6.3, we show three focal subblocks. They are designated as—

L. *Member's share of profit, loss, and capital,*
M. *Member's share of liabilities at end of year, and*
N. *Member's capital account analysis.*

These items play a dominant role when formulating a written *Operating Agreement* for the LLC. We'll address this matter more pointedly in our upcoming Chapter 11: LLC Operation Agreement. Our position is that, without a clearly-worded operating agreement, a multi-member LLC will — at some point — careen suddenly into a sham entity controlled by con artists and self promoters.

Also, recall earlier that there are two classes of LLC membership. One class is an: *LLC member-manager*; the other class is an: *Other LLC member.* The operating agreement is supposed to clarify the distinction between the two classes, and what the rights are of other members who disagree with the managing member(s). There is also the issue of each member's voting rights. Should such rights be proportional to the amount of net capital that each member has on the line? For tax and financial matters "Yes"; for policy matters "No".

Part III of Figure 6.3 is a digest of the 40 or so specific types of pass-through dollars. Here again, the operating agreement comes into focus with respect to each member's relative profits, losses, credits, capital exposure, deductions, and liabilities.

Part IV is a blank space labeled: *For IRS Use Only.* What do you suppose this space is for?

Answer: It is for each IRS screener who examines Form 1065 and its K-1s attached, to flag each K-1 that appears to be out of line or inconsistent with that member's capital investment. In other words, the Part IV blank space in Figure 6.3 is for "red flagging" that LLC member whom the IRS deems is abusing the distributive-sharing process. If 50% or more of the members are so deemed, the LLC itself will be designated as an abusive tax sheltering device. Then IRS penalties can be assessed.

The K-1 Origin: Schedule K

Schedule K-1 does not evolve until after page 3 of Form 1065 is complete. The full length of page 3 is Schedule K, titled: *Partners'* (substitute *Members'*) *Distributive Share Items*. Note with special care that Schedule K is **plural**: Members' . . . whereas Schedule K-1 is *singular*: Member's. The placement of the apostrophe (s' or 's) makes a world of difference. In the aggregate, there is an amount called: "members' capital" which, generally, is the target for liability lawsuits. Thus, an adversary is more interested in Schedule K (which is a single document) than in rummaging through a handful of individual member documents: the K-1s and their pass-through instructions.

Schedule K (the one with the s') summarizes the membership pass-through tax items that derive from all books, records, and activities of the LLC entity for the year. The line numbers and line captions on Schedule K correspond identically with those on Schedule K-1 (the one with the 's). In this manner, whatever entry amount is on a line on Schedule K appears, with modification, on its corresponding line on Schedule K-1. The "modification" is *each member's percentage* of profit sharing, loss sharing, and ownership of capital (as appropriate).

For example, if a line entry on Schedule K showed $1,286 and a particular member's percentage interest was 17.76%, the amount transferred to that member's Schedule K-1 would be—

$1,286 x 0.1776 = $228 (rounded).

Imagine having 10 LLC members, each with a different percentage of sharing, and a Schedule K with eight entry amounts on it. This would require the preparation of 10 Schedules K-1. Each such K-1 would have eight different entries of fractioned amounts from Schedule K. That would be 80 separate computations to be made. What if there were 100 LLC members? (That would be 800 computations.) The accompanying accounting tasks require extraordinary backup worksheets to placate any skeptical K-1 recipient. Unless all LLC members familiarize themselves with the K-1 process (as we depict in Figure 6.4), one recalcitrant recipient — he who demands a single, simple, bottom-line amount — could cause all other members to be late in receiving their K-1s. Any K-1 lateness, in turn, causes each recipient to be late when filing his own individual Form 1040.

Who prepares the Schedule K?

Answer: The *Tax Matters Member* (TMM). Such a person should be of the member-manager class who is astute enough to engage professional talent when needed. The completion of Form 1065 with all attachments would come under the TMM's supervision. He/she would be like a CFO (chief financial officer) in a large corporation. As such, the TMM would be responsible for oversight of all tax and financial records, including the sufficiency of the capital accounts of all LLC members.

Net Income or <Loss>

After preparing Schedule K, the next task for the TMM is to establish the net income or net loss for the year. To do so, the TMM starts with page 1 of Form 1065 and records the bottom line thereto. Said line is captioned: *Ordinary business income <loss>*. Page 1 is a 22-line Income and Expense Statement for the principal (core) business of the LLC. Those members participating in this activity are tax characterized as either: (a) material participants, or (b) passive participants. Material (nonpassive) participants are those who essentially run the business on a day-to-day basis. The prorata income attributed to their participation is subject to self-employment tax. Any prorata net losses attributable to passive participants are subject to loss limitation rules. This was the textual reference to Form 6198 (At-Risk Limitations) and to Form 8582 (Passive Activity Loss Rules) on page 6-7.

There are also supplemental activities that contribute to the overall net income or net loss of the LLC enterprise. These are mostly investment-type activities where material personal participation is not dominant. Such activities consist of:

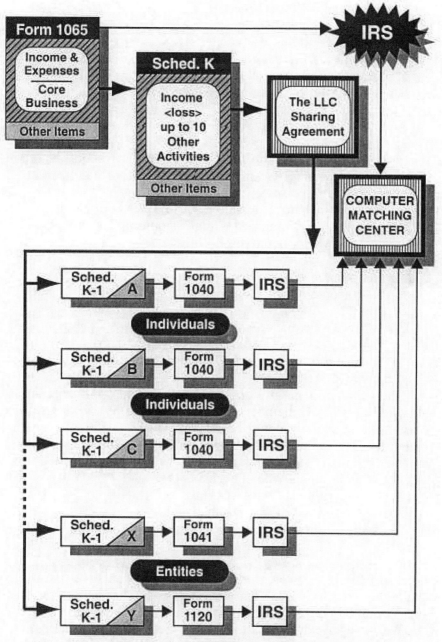

Fig. 6.4 - The K-1 Pass-Through Process for Multi-Member LLCs

1. Net rental real estate income <loss>
2. Other net rental income <loss>
3. Dividend and interest income
4. Royalties (from natural resources)
5. Net short-term capital gain <loss>
6. Net long-term capital gain <loss>
7. Other gain <loss> (from sale of business assets)
8. Other income <loss> (attach statement)

As to item 8, the instruction to Schedule K lists about 10 other sources of income. These include real estate mortgage conduits, cancellation of debt, disposition of farm property, etc.

The instructions to Schedule K also list about 20 items of deductions allowable against the total income or loss above. The result is net income or net loss as follows:

A. Net income <loss> from core business _____
B. Net income <loss> from supplemental activities _____
C. Combine A and B.................................▶ _____
D. Allowable deductions from Schedule K <_____>
    Subtract D from C to arrive at:
E. **Total net income** (or **total net loss**) for the year _____

Once the amount at Item E is established, said amount is allocated to all LLC members by type. Form 1065 (at top of page 4) suggests that there could be as many as 12 different types of members. The most important types for our purposes are—

Active individuals (member-managers)
Active individuals (other LLC members)
Passive individuals (member-managers)
Passive individuals (other LLC members)

All other members are entity types, such as: (1) partnerships, (2) other LLCs, (3) S corporations, (4) decedents' estates, (5) gratuitous trusts, (6) exempt organizations (charitables, pension trusts, municipalities), (7) C corporations, and (8) foreign entities.

We have just described to you, in more expansive terms, the true meaning of a "multi-member LLC." Having so many different types of members can create internal problems of their own, especially if the dominant capital contributor is an entity. Entity members rarely participate in the core business activities.

To avoid careening out of operational and financial control, the number of individual (human being) members should always be greater than the number of entity members. While entity members can contribute the greater portion of operating capital, their participative interest is limited to two objectives: (1) income growth, **or** (2) tax shelter losses. If these objectives are not met, the entity members themselves could become your first serious litigants in a liability lawsuit.

The Allure of Form 1065

Neither Schedule K nor any of the Schedules K-1 is signed by anyone. Being part of Form 1065, they are authenticated by the signature(s) appearing at the bottom of its page 1. The principal signature is that of the general manager who must be an LLC member. If the return is prepared professionally, the preparer's signature also appears. Both signatures follow a jurat clause: *Under penalties of perjury . . .* that Form 1065 *. . . including accompanying schedules and statements . . . is true, correct, and complete . . .* to the best of each signer's knowledge.

Otherwise, the bulk of page 1 is a straightforward profit and loss statement. A preprinted **Caution** states: *Include **only** trade or business income and expenses.* Some 22 lines are preprinted for this purpose. There is an **Income** portion, with line 8 captioned: **Total income (loss)**. There is a **Deductions** portion, with line 21 captioned: **Total deductions**. Line 22 is full captioned:

Ordinary business income <loss>. *Subtract line 21 from line 8.* [Enter here and on Schedule K at line 1.]

Believe this or not: The line 22, page 1, is the **only information** transferred from Form 1065 to Schedule K. As indicated above, it goes onto line 1 of Schedule K. The caption for that line of Schedule K is identical to that above. This is followed by the parenthetical notation (from *page 1, line 22* of Form 1065). We also add that the same caption: Ordinary business income

<loss> appears as line 1 on each member's Schedule K-1. All the K-1 lines must equal the total amount on line 1, Schedule K.

There is a line 2 and some 44 other lines on Schedule K. Where does their information come from? It comes from other forms and schedules that attach to Schedule K. For example, line 2 on Schedule K reads—

Net income (loss) from rental real estate activities. (Attach Form 8825).

Form 8825: What's that? Its title is: ***Rental Real Estate Income and Expenses of a Partnership*** [LLC] ***or an S corporation.***

Other lines on Schedule K (not all) carry preprinted instructions to attach specific forms or schedules. Those lines absent preprinted instructions derive their information from the ***Specific Instructions to Schedules K and K-1*** (some 12 to 20 pages of text).

Here, now, we have revealed the tax mechanics of a little-known fact. Because, by design, Schedule K is automatically part of Form 1065, it accommodates any number of different activities engaged in by a multi-member LLC. There is no statutory limit. The allure of such flexibility is truly fascinating.

The Balance Sheets

No other tax document describes the financial health of an LLC better than its balance sheets. There is a balance sheet for the beginning of the year and, separately, one for the end of the year. Differences between the balance sheets from one year to the next represent either growth, stagnation, or decline of the enterprise. A balance sheet, as you know, is a statement of the assets, liabilities, and capital of an entity. Such information is not part of Schedule K nor of Schedule K-1.

There is a separate schedule of its own for listing the assets and liabilities of an LLC. It is **Schedule L**: ***Balance Sheets per Books***. This schedule takes up half of page 4 of Form 1065. The instructions for Schedule L say—

The balance sheets should agree with the [LLC's] *books and records. Attach a statement explaining any differences.*

SCHEDULE L	BALANCE SHEETS	- Beginning of Year [Cols. (a) & (b)] - End of Year [Cols. (c) & (d)]	
	ASSETS	**(c)**	**(d)**
1	Cash	▨	
2a	Accounts receivable		▨
b	**LESS** allowances for bad debts		
3	Inventories	▨	
4	U.S. Government obligations	▨	
5	Tax-exempt securities	▨	
6	Other current assets	▨	
7	Mortgage & real estate loans	▨	
8	Other investments	▨	
9a	Buildings & other depreciable assets		▨
b	**LESS** accumulated depreciation		
10a	Depletable assets		▨
b	**LESS** accumulated depreciation		
11	Land	▨	
12a	Intangible assets		▨
b	**LESS** accumulated amortization		
13	Other assets	▨	
14	**Total Assets**	▨	
	LIABILITIES & CAPITAL	▨	▨
15	Accounts payable	▨	
16	Mortgages, notes payable < 1 year	▨	
17	Other current liabilities	▨	
18	**ALL nonrecourse loans**	▨	
19	Mortgages, notes payable > 1 year	▨	
20	Other liabilities	▨	
21	**Members' capital accounts**	▨	
22	**Total Liabilities & Capital**	▨	
	Attach explanations	▨	

Fig. 6.5 - Edited/Abbreviated End-of-Year LLC Balance Sheet

We present in Figure 6.5 an abridged (and slightly edited) replica of Schedule L (Form 1065). Note that we only show *End of year* columns and omit those for *Beginning of year.*

We urge that you take a moment and read down each of the 26 line items in Figure 6.5. Such reading alone is instructive in that it gives you a feel for why we believe Schedule L is so important. It gives you a snapshot of the financial health of a multi-member LLC. Line 21: **Members' capital accounts** capstones it all. The dollar amount there must be significantly greater than zero..

Technically, if total receipts are less than $250,000 **and** total assets (at end of year) are less than $600,000, no Schedule L is IRS required. It takes a lot of work to get the balance sheets in balance. Not doing so, even when not required, inevitably raises suspicions about the accounting discipline, management efficiency, and financial health of the LLC. Without the balance sheets, members tend to argue among themselves, creditors worry about being paid, and plaintiffs' attorneys see an opening for the kill. Having no balance sheets tends to destroy the legitimacy of the protective shield against the personal liability of LLC members. A balance sheet establishes the members' collective net worth.

On the liabilities side of the balancing effort, there is one item that requires close attention and control. It is item 18 (in Figure 6.5): **All nonrecourse loans.** A nonrecourse loan is a liability of the entity for which no LLC member bears the economic risk of loss. Lacking this member risk, there is temptation to wheel and deal at the entity level without serious concentration on growing the business and its net worth. Because total liabilities and capital must equal total assets, it should be self-evident that the greater the amount of nonrecourse loans, the less the LLC members' capital accounts. Low capital accounts imply a cavalier attitude towards the entire LLC operation.

Capital Accounts Reconciliation

On Schedule L, there is no direct, stand-alone entry item for the impact of net income or loss from an LLC's year-long operation. It appears indirectly in the members' capital accounts. We display this indirection for you in Figure 6.6. Start at the bottom of the figure and follow the bold arrows up.

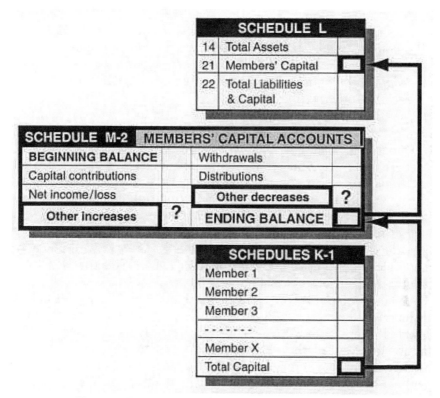

Fig. 6.6 - The Pivotal Balancing Role of Schedule M-2

The "indirection" is several reconciliation steps between Schedule K (not shown in Figure 6.6) and Schedule L. For starters, there is a subschedule insert just above Schedule L which is captioned: *Analysis of Net Income (Loss)*. By following the preprinted instructions thereon, an *aggregate* net income or loss for the entity overall is established.

Below Schedule L, there is a Schedule M-2 titled: *Analysis of Members' Capital Accounts*. Schedule M-2 plays the pivotal role in the whole reconciliation and balancing process. As you can sense from the depiction in Figure 6.6, there is a delicate interlock between the LLC members' *aggregate* capital accounts (Schedule M-2) and the individual accounts displayed on Schedules K-1, all of which in turn appear as one combined item (line 21) on Schedule L. To achieve the perfect interlock, a lot of trial and error juggling goes on. The instructions to Schedule M-2 say—

> *The amounts of Schedule M-2 should equal the total of the amounts reported in **item** N of all the partners' [LLC members'] Schedules K-1. . . . If the capital balances differ from the amounts reported on Schedule L, attach a statement reconciling any differences.*

Item N on Schedule K-1 is a near-replica of Schedule M-2 for each LLC member, separately.

Perhaps, now, you realize why Schedule L: **Balance Sheets per Books**, is so important to the tax and legal credibility of an LLC. Having no such schedule, or having one that is incomplete (re Schedule M-1: **Reconciliation of Income (Loss) per Books with Income (Loss) per Return** and Schedule M-2), raises questions about the correctness of the K-1s. Any absence or incompleteness on page 4 of Form 1065 (where Schedule L is) is a natural magnet for personal liability lawsuits.

When books, records, and financial statements are poorly maintained, general negligence is often the first cause of action asserted against an LLC. The term "negligence" refers to the failure to exercise the degree of care that a person of ordinary prudence would exercise under the same circumstances. Gross negligence carries the degree of inattention further. Gross negligence is the intentional or willful failure to perform a clear duty by recklessly disregarding the consequences of injury to person or property that attend such failure. Forthrightly stated, the "LL" shield is not a panacea for failing to act responsibly in a trade, profession, or business. Nor can Form 1065 be signed cavalierly while ignoring the *Under penalties of perjury* clause.

7

CALIFORNIA'S LLC FORM

California Has Its Own "Return Of Income" Tax Form For LLCs Doing Business Within Its Borders, Whether Organized In State Or Out of State. The Reason: California Imposes An LLC Tax, An LLC Franchise Fee, And Withholds Income Tax On Nonconsenting NONRESIDENT Members. Integral With Its Form Are Schedules K And K-1 For Distributive Share Items. These Schedules Start With Federal Amounts, Adjust For California Differences, And Apply An APPORTIONMENT FORMULA To Arrive At California SOURCE Amounts From A Mixture Of Multi-State Income. The California Form Is Highly Instructive.

General partnerships and ordinary proprietorships require no "licensing" by the Secretary of State where the business is organized and conducted. Each such entity can start a profit-seeking activity in good faith, abide by the general business code of the state . . . and that's it. There is no periodic certification, filing, or licensing fee involved. Why so?

Simple answer. There is no statutory liability protection for general partnerships and sole proprietorships. The owners of these forms of business are personally liable for wrongful acts, regardless of whatever capital base they maintain.

When it comes to an LLC entity, whether a partnership LLC (multi-member) or a proprietorship LLC (single member), all states impose a "fee" of some kind. The fee is for the filing, certification, and updating of the Articles of Organization and the

LLC's List of Managers. Beyond this, income tax matters are handled by a separate agency of the state. Not all states, however, impose income taxes. There are nine states that do not. (We'll list these nine states later.)

California takes the tax and fee business to a new level. In addition to the Secretary of State's fee, California's Franchise Tax Board imposes an LLC tax AND an LLC fee. These are **in addition to** the income tax imposed on LLC members individually. Furthermore, the LLC tax and LLC fee apply equally to partnership LLCs and proprietorship LLCs. All of which justifies, in California, a quite different tax form for LLCs. This is Form 568: *Limited Liability Company Return of Income*.

Accordingly, in this chapter, we want to acquaint you with the more significant features of California's Form 568, and how it applies to both partnership LLCs and proprietorship LLCs. Also, we want to acquaint you with how Form 568 applies to both resident and nonresident members, whether individual or entity. California imposes stringent apportionment rules between in-state and out-of-state sources of income. These rules apply regardless of whether an LLC is organized in California or outside of California doing business in California. Thus, we think the California LLC form is instructive, if for no other reason than to compare it with the state in which you do business as an LLC. We think it is also instructive to see how California treats LLCs differently from the way the IRS treats LLCs.

California's "Tax on Tax"

As we tried to convey in the previous chapter (re multi-member LLCs), there is no federal tax imposed on an LLC at the entity level. The reason for the federal "no entity tax" is that all net income, net loss, credits, and certain deductions, etc. are passed through to entity members who are separately income taxed. The same income tax pass-through principle applies to California LLCs. But, there's a difference. As we have alluded to above, there are, additionally, an entity tax and an entity fee.

California treats an LLC for franchise purposes just like it treats a corporation. It imposes both a franchise tax **and** a franchise fee for the privilege of doing business in California.

Neither of these two franchise impositions is regarded as an income tax, though they are based on income in the general sense. The LLC franchise tax is a flat $800 each year. It applies whether the LLC generates profit, loss, or not, or whether it generates any income at all. This is for starters.

California also imposes an LLC franchise fee based on total income for the year. For fee purposes, the term total income is based on the grand total **positive** income (**before** cost of goods, expenses, allowances) generated by the LLC in California. No losses whatsoever are taken into account. For example, on the matter of capital gains and losses involving business activities, the Form 568 instructions say—

14a. *Enter the capital gains (**not losses**) of disregarded entities* [single member LLCs in proprietorship form].

14b. *Enter LLC's distributive share of capital gains (**not losses**) from pass-through entities* [partnerships, other LLCs, S corporations, trusts].

14c. *Enter the capital gains (**not losses**) included on Schedule D (568)* [Capital Gain or Loss].

California has a 36-line worksheet for computing an LLC's total income. The above example is just three lines of the 36. By not considering any otherwise allowable offsets against total income, there is no computed taxable income. Consequently, the rationale is that any amount imposed on total income is not a tax: it is a franchise fee. It is a license for the sole privilege of doing business in California. As fee rates go, it is not onerous: about 2/10ths of 1 percent (0.2%). There is no LLC fee for total incomes of less than $250,000. For total incomes between $250,000 and $5,000,000, the LLC fee ranges from $1,000 to $6,000. For total incomes over $5,000,000, the LLC fee is $9,000+. In our mind, this is another tax on income. There's still more.

If a California LLC has nonresident members — either out-of-state or out-of-country — the entity must withhold California income taxes from each such member's distributive share. The year 2005 withholding rates, for example, were 1.5% for S corporations, 8.8% for C corporations, and 9.3% for individuals, partnerships, LLCs, and fiduciaries. If a nonresident member consents in writing to California's jurisdiction over his distributive share, and promises to file a California nonresident income tax return, no withholding by the LLC entity is required.

Altogether, an LLC in California has the following financial burdens beyond those required on a federal LLC return:

LLC franchise tax	$800 annually
LLC franchise fee	0.2% of total income (approximately)
Nonresident withholdings	9+% of each member's distributive share

We don't know about you, but this appears to us like a "tax on tax." Hence, the observation: California is an egregious taxing state.

Overview of Form 568

We are quite aware that California's Form 568 may not be of direct interest to those readers who are LLC participants in states other than California. Nevertheless, we think that a quick skim-through will cause you to appreciate better your blessings. At the same time, you'll be on notice that a non-California LLC doing business in California will be subject to a nonresident tax imposed by California.

California's Form 568: *Limited Liability Company Return of Income*, consists of four pages. Additionally, there are numerous attachments (forms and schedules) where applicable. Its page 1 consists of the following categories:

1. Head portion — name, address, type of activity, etc.
2. Information portion — 15 Yes/No checkboxes
3. LLC tax and fee summary
4. Single member consent portion
5. Signature portion — officer or member, and preparer

We'll come back to the most significant features of page 1, shortly.

Page 2 of Form 568 consists of the following schedules:

A — **Cost of Goods Sold**
B — **Income and Deductions**
T — **Nonconsenting Nonresident Members' Tax Liability**

Schedules A and B are not significantly different from similar schedules for proprietorships, partnerships, or corporations. These schedules address an ordinary trade or business, where one or more LLC members actively participate. Schedule T consists of four columns: (1) Member's name, (2) Member's federal Tax I.D., (3) Distributive share of income x tax rate, and (4) Member's tax due. Schedule T cannot be prepared until all distributed sharing has been prorata fractioned.

The entire page 3 of Form 568 is Schedule K: *Members'* [plural] *Shares of Income, Deductions, Credits, Etc.* With the exception of self-employment tax and foreign taxes (which do not apply in California), this schedule is near-identical to the federal Schedule K(1065). However, whereas the K(1065) involves two columnar amounts, the K(568) requires three columnar amounts:

Col. (a) — Amounts from federal K(1065)
Col. (b) — California adjustments
Col. (c) — Total amounts using California law

Page 4 of Form 568 consists of the following schedules:

L — *Balance Sheets*
 • Assets • Liabilities • Capital
M-1 — *Reconciliation of Income per Books*
 With Income per Return
M-2 — *Analysis of Members' Capital Accounts*
O — *Amounts from Liquidation Used to Capitalize a*
 Limited Liability Company

Schedules L, M-1, an M-2 are line-for-line identical with these corresponding schedules on federal Form 1065 (partnership). Instructions caution: *Use California amounts.* The preprinted instructions at Schedule O are self-explanatory. What California is looking for here are any predecessor businesses that were liquidated to form the LLC, and whether the liquidation gains (if any) were tax recognized in California . . . or elsewhere. The IRS, as well as California, wants to be apprised of potential abusive tax practices when "switching businesses around."

Page 1, Form 568 Revisited

The head portion of California Form 568 for LLCs requires virtually the same descriptive information as does federal Form 1065 for partnerships. Such information includes: Principal business activity; principal product or service; date business started; total assets at end of year; method of accounting: cash, accrual, or other. Additionally, there is a space entry (top, upper right) for: *Secretary of State file number.* This, of course, is for the coordination of administrative and legal matters between the Secretary of State and the California Franchise Tax Board.

Of the general information block, the first box space there (double wide) is item J. It reads—

> *Enter the maximum number of members in the LLC at any time during the year. Attach a California Schedule K-1(568) for each of these members.*

At this point, you become aware that there is a California Schedule K-1: **Member's** [singular] **Share of Income, Deductions, Credits,** *etc.* It is quite similar to the federal K-1. In the California K-1, in addition to the distributive share column (a), there are columns—

> *(b)   Amounts from federal K-1(1065)*
> *(c)   California adjustments*
> *(d)   Total amounts using California law*
> *(e)   California source amounts* [when col. (d) includes amounts from non-California sources]

Of the 15 Yes/No checkboxes following item J, most are reasonably self-explanatory. There are a few information stoppers, however. For example, item L asks—

> *Is this LLC apportioning income to California using Schedule R? [**Apportionment and Allocation of Income**]* ☐ Yes ☐ No

We'll come back to Schedule R, below. The main body of page 1 of Form 568 — and probably its real reason for existence — is its LLC tax and fee portion. This portion is so significant that we replicate it (abbreviated where necessary) in Figure 7.1

Form 568	LIMITED LIABILITY COMPANY RETURN OF INCOME	Year
Head Portion Yes/No Checkboxes	State File No. _____ Date Started _____ Total Assets _____	

	1	Total income from worksheet	
	2	LLC FEE - see instructions	
	3	LLC TAX - see instructions	
	4	Nonconsenting NR members' tax liability	
	5	TOTAL TAX AND FEE. Add the above	
	6	Payment vouchers; Extension vouchers;	
	7	Overpayment credits; Withholding credits	
	8	Nonresident withholding credit	
	9	Total payments. Add 6, 7, and 8	
	10	Tax & fee due. Subtract 9 from 5	
	11	Overpayment (if any)	
	12	To be credited or refunded	
	13	Use tax (on out-state purchases)	
	14	Penalties & interest - see instructions	
	15	AMOUNT DUE - - - - - - - - - ⟶	

Enclose . . . Any Payment (left vertical side caption)

Single Member Consent
Jurat Clause & Signatures

Fig. 7.1 - LLC Levies for the Privilege of Doing Business in California

We urge that you take a moment and read down all 15 line captions in the above figure. California is clearly gunning for nonresident LLC members, and for those resident members who purchase goods out of state for use within state. Also note the left-hand vertical side caption: ***Enclose . . . any payment.*** This side caption alone tells you why California wants a totally separate LLC tax return of its own.

Single Member LLCs

Whereas we have referred federally to single member LLCs as either an LLC proprietorship or a solo S corporation, California refers to them as **SMLLCs** or disregarded entities (the "SM" is single member). The first indication of separate treatment of SMLLCs on Form 568 is item U. This two-part question reads—

U(1) *Is this LLC a business entity disregarded for tax purposes?* ☐ *Yes* ☐ *No*

U(2) *If yes, see instructions and complete Page 1 and Page 3 only. Are there credits or credit carryovers attributable to the disregarded entity?* ☐ *Yes* ☐ *No*

The "see instructions" refers to federal Form 8832: Entity Classification Election (recall Chapter 4) by requiring that a copy of it be attached to California Form 568.

About four inches below item U(2), there is a SMLLC portion which reads:

Single Member LLC Information and Consent
— Complete only if the LLC is disregarded.

The instruction here means that, if the SMLLC has opted for a solo S corporation (federal Form 1120S), the consent statement is not required. Otherwise, the SMLLC cites his company's name, federal Tax ID, and Secretary of State file number, then signs (on page 1) the following consent statement:

I consent to the jurisdiction of the State of California to tax my LLC income and agree to file returns and pay tax as may be required by the Franchise Tax Board.

The most likely California returns for a SMLLC would be—

Form 540 — *California Resident Income Tax Return*
Form 540NR — *California Nonresident or Part-Year Resident Income Tax Return*

Page 3 of Form 568 is Schedule K: distributive share items. In a SMLLC, there is no distributive sharing. All 100% of each item on Schedule K(568) goes to the sole owner. This means that for Column (b): *Amounts from federal K(1065)*, one strikes out those words and prints above them: SMLLC. He then goes through all of the federal forms he has filed, and enters onto the K(568) all of the matching items he can find.

Analysis: Schedule K (568)

For multi-member LLCs, Schedule K(568) is the driving force for the reconciliation efforts of Schedule M-1: ***Income per Books with Income per Return***. The California instructions to Schedule K(568) say—

> *See federal instructions for Schedule K: Analysis of Net Income (Loss)* . . . [for arriving at] ***Total distributive income payment items*** [the "bottom line"].

Whereas Schedule K(568) has some 40 or so possible entry amounts, by following the preprinted *Combine . . . subtract* instructions in its analysis portion, one summary amount is posted. There are 7+ "combine" lines and 6+ "subtract" lines. Each is expressly identified in the *Analysis* portion of K(568). With the exception of long-term capital gain and credit for foreign taxes paid (which California does not recognize), the "combine and subtract" lines are identical for the K(1065) and K(568). With one total distributive amount, the analysis of members begins.

We do our best in Figure 7.2 to schematize what is taking place at the "bottom line" of Schedule K. Credits and carryovers are not included. They are addressed on separate tax forms of their own.

The "analysis" of Schedule K is the apportionment of the total distributive amount to each type of member: individual, corporation, partnership, LLC, trust, etc. The analysis does not address the number of members; we get this from the number of Schedules K-1 attached. The analysis addresses the type of member: individual or entity, and the distributive dollar amount to each class type. If there are more individual than entity members, it implies greater profit-seeking devotion.

Sched. K (568) : Members' Shares of Distributive Items			
Listed Items	Federal Amounts	California Adjustments	California Amounts
			●
			●
● COMBINE designated items			●
☐ SUBTRACT designated items			☐
			☐

Total Distributive Income/Payments Items				▬ ▬ ▬ ▬ ▬ ▶		$ Net Total Amount	
$ Amount to each member class	Individual		Corpor-ation	Partner-ship	LLC	Other
	Active	Passive				
Near-identical to items on federal Schedule K (1065)							

Fig. 7.2 - Analysis Taking Place at Bottom of Schedule K (568)

Where a member is an individual, he must be classified as "active" or "passive." This is because passive members are subject to special loss limitation rules, which active/nonpassive members are not. For this classification effort, the federal instructions to K(1065) — which California follows — say, in paraphrased terms:

An LLC should classify each member as "active or passive" to the best of its knowledge and belief. In most cases, the level of participation in an activity will be apparent. If not apparent or readily determinable, classify the member as "passive."

The IRS is more interested in those members who actively (materially) participate in the LLC business than is California, because of the federal system of social security and medicare tax.

Nonresident Members: List of

Like most other income taxing states, California is very sensitive about nonresidents earning money from California sources. One can appreciate this sensitivity when being informed that the bulk of an LLC's organizational and operating capital could be contributed by out-of-state members. Whether the nonresident members are individuals or entities, they could reside in any of the nine non-income-taxing states! Worse yet, there are tax problems when LLC members reside outside of the U.S. Now you know one of the reasons why the analysis-of-members portion of Schedule K is so important.

Editorial Note: The nine non-income-taxing states are: (1) Alaska, (2) Florida, (3) Nevada, (4) New Hampshire, (5) South Dakota, (6) Tennessee, (7) Texas, (8) Washington, and (9) Wyoming.

Because of nonresidency problems with the collection of its tax, California has promulgated **Form 3832**. Its title is: *Limited Liability Company's List of* [Nonresident] *Members and Consents*. If not already self-evident, the purpose of this form is—

1. To list the names and Tax IDs of all LLC members who are not residents of California;

2. To obtain the signatures, where possible, of those nonresidents who consent to the tax jurisdiction of California;

3. To list separately those nonresidents who have sold or transferred their ownership interests during the current year; and

4. To "flag" those who fail to sign the consent statement by requiring the LLC to withhold tax on that member's distributive amount at his highest marginal rate.

For its informative benefit, we present in Figure 7.3 a condensed version of Form 3832. The bulk of the condensation pertains to the various small-print instructions thereon. The consent statement (indicated in bold) is separately cited below.

Form 3832	LIST OF NONRESIDENT MEMBERS & CONSENTS			Year
LLC Name	State File No. _____ Fed. Tax I.D. No. _____			

///	**List Members of Record at End of Taxable Year**			
	Name	**CONSENT STATEMENT**		Tax I.D.
		Signature	Date	
1				
2				
3				
4				
5				
etc.				

///	**List Those Who Sold or Transferred Ownership Interests**			
	Name	**CONSENT STATEMENT**		Tax I.D.
		Signature	Date	
1				
2				
3				
etc.				

Fig. 7.3 - General Arrangement of List for Nonresident Member Consents

Immediately below the title, a headnote reads—

For use by LLCs with one or more nonresident members. Attach to Form 568 and give a copy to each nonresident member. Use additional sheet(s) if necessary.

In the signature column, the consent statement reads—

Only nonresident members must sign: *"I consent to the jurisdiction of the State of California to tax my distributive share of the LLC income attributable to California sources."*

There is also a caution on Form 3832. Every recipient is informed that by signing the form the nonresident is not relieved of his/her/their/its obligation to file California nonresident or part-year resident returns. California bases its filing requirements on the principle of: ***Gross income from all sources***. The term "all sources" means (a) within California, (b) outside of California but within the U.S., and (c) outside of the U.S., if so much as $1 is earned from a business in California. The overall consequence is that if an LLC member has to file a federal return and gets an LLC distributive share from California, he'll have to file a California return, whether resident or not.

Source Determination Rules

When business income is derived from sources both within and outside of the state, it becomes necessary to determine the portion attributable to California sources. The situation is the same for other business-taxing and income-taxing states. This is a reciprocal agreement among affected states that have adopted the Uniform Division of Income Act for Tax Purposes and the Multistate Tax Compact. The idea is to avoid double taxation on the same income generated in one state and distributed to a member in another state, with each state claiming full taxing authority over such income.

The source determination (origin of income rules) addresses business income and nonbusiness income separately. The term "business income" is directed at a trade or business where extensive personal services are performed on a regular, continuous, and substantial basis. "Nonbusiness income" constitutes all else. Nonbusiness income includes that from real and tangible property (buildings, equipment, vehicles) and from intangible property (bank accounts, stock portfolios, pensions, annuities, royalties).

We summarize in Figure 7.4 the uniform source determination rules. They are "uniform" among the states . . . except for California. Whereas most states use a 3-factor apportionment formula, California uses a 4-factor formula. California does this with **Schedule R** (in Figure 7.4) titled: ***Apportionment and Allocation of Income***. The term "apportionment" means — *the division of business income among states by use of an apportionment formula*. The term "allocation" means— *the assignment of nonbusiness income to a particular state*. Real and tangible property is sourced to the state of its physical presence;

intangible property is sourced to the state of each taxpayer's primary residence.

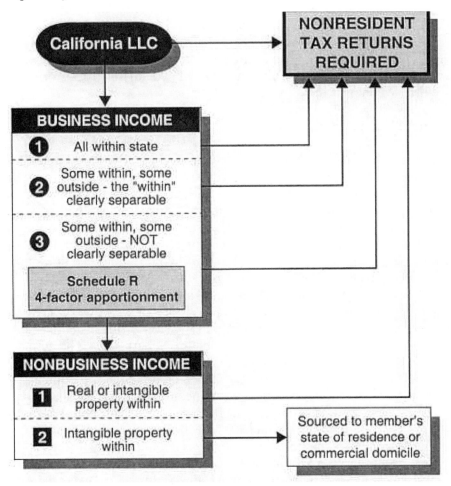

Fig. 7.4 - Source-of-Income Rules for Nonresident Members of Calif. LLC

The standard apportionment formula consists of: (1) a property factor (both real and tangible); (2) a payroll factor (all forms of compensation for personal services rendered); and (3) a sales factor (all gross receipts from the sale of tangible and intangible property). California deviates from this standard by applying a "double-weighted" sales factor. The result is—

$$\left[\frac{\text{Calif. prop.}}{\text{Total prop.}} + \frac{\text{Calif. payroll}}{\text{Total payroll}} + \frac{2 \times \text{Calif. sales}}{\text{Total sales}} \right] \div 4$$

= California Apportionment

The apportionment factor is applied to California-adjusted federal amounts to arrive at a *California source amount.*

Effect on Schedule K-1(568)

From our earlier comments, you are already aware that each member of an LLC conducting business in California receives a Schedule K-1 (Form 568). This is that *Member's Share of* . . . distributive income/payment items. In almost every respect except self-employment and foreign tax items, the federal K-1(1065) and the California K-1(568) are item-by-item comparable. The big differences are the number of columns and their headings, and the computational assumptions used by California. The K-1(568) assumes that each LLC member is a California resident, unless the following question is answered "Yes":

Is this member a nonresident of California? ☐ Yes ☐ No

The K-1(568) instructions direct that the federal K-1(1065) be used only to prepare column (b) of the K-1(568). The column (b) is captioned: *Amounts from federal K-1(1065).* Thereafter the K-1(1065) is set aside and the instructions for K-1(568) are to be followed. The LLC is required to furnish each member a copy of the instructions, or at least provide instructions on each item-amount entered in column (b). The column (c) is captioned: *California adjustments.*

The transcriptional focus in Schedule K-1(568) is its columns (d) and (e). Column (d) is captioned: *Total amounts using California law.* This column is a combination of columns (b): federal amounts and (c): California adjustments. Column (d) is based on the assumption that — temporarily — all members are California residents. This assumption puts all source determinations (origin of income) on common ground. Then column (e) is derived by applying source determination rules (as explained above). Column (e) is captioned: *California source amounts and credits*.

The instructions to column (e) say—

> *Column (e) includes **only** income, deductions, gains, or losses that are ... **sourced to California**. The residency of a member [at this point] is not a factor in the amounts to be included in columns (d) and (e). . . . For an LLC doing business wholly within California, columns (d) and (e) will generally be the same . . . except for **nonbusiness intangible income**.* [Emphasis added.]

Nonbusiness intangible income is sourced to the state of residence of a member individual, or to the commercial domicile of a member entity.

If you are a member individual of a non-California LLC doing business in California, you are in for a personal income tax shock. Say you live in a non-income-taxing state. As such, you still have to pay California personal income tax via its Form 540NR: *California Nonresident or Part-Year Resident Income Tax*. Check the website: **www.ftb.ca.gov,** and pull up Form 540NR and its 50 pages of instructions. When you do, you'll promptly decide to become a NONCONSENTING Nonresident on Form 568. This will cost you 9.3% of your California source distributive share. If your share is $1,000 or less, the tax highjacking (of less than $100) by California would not be too burdensome.

8

FOREIGN ENTITY LLCs

A Foreign LLC Is An Unincorporated Entity Created And Organized Under Foreign Law. Through A U.S. Manager, It Can Elect Its Form Of Tax Treatment When Conducting A Trade Or Business In The U.S. The Most Common Such Treatment Is That Of A Partnership Where The "Pass-Through" Principles Of Distributive Sharing With Foreign Members Apply. At The End Of A Foreign LLC's Tax Accounting Year, Stringent WITHHOLDING AT SOURCE Rules Apply. The Idea Is To Over-Withhold Tax So As To "Dollar Carrot" Each Foreign LLC Member To File For A Refund, By Using Form 1040NR: U.S. Nonresident Alien Income Tax Return.

For LLC purposes, an "eligible entity" — whether domestic or foreign — is a for-profit business which is not a corporation. A domestic entity is one created or organized in the U.S., or under a law of the U.S., or under a law of any state of the U.S. An entity is foreign if it is not domestic. Not all foreign entities, however, are eligible for LLC treatment. IRS Regulation § 301.7701-2(b)(8) lists some 80+ foreign entities as *per se corporations.* The "per se" means having more characteristics of a U.S. corporation than those of an unincorporated U.S. enterprise. Except for the IRS listed per se entities, all other business arrangements of foreign origin are eligible for LLC treatment under U.S. tax laws.

Foreign entities conducting LLC business within the U.S. are subject to U.S. tax laws under two commonly recognized international taxation principles. One principle addresses that income which is *effectively connected with* a trade or business in the U.S. The entity and owners are subject to the same tax rates and benefits as are U.S. citizens and domestic LLCs. The second principle addresses that income which is *fixed or determinable from* sources within the U.S. (from other than a trade or business). The fixed or determinable income is taxed at a flat 30% rate, or at a lower rate if there is a Tax Treaty in effect. The U.S. has entered into agreements with some 65+ sovereign nations with the objective of minimizing any double taxation to those foreign citizens and entities. Such is an "objective" only.

Accordingly, in this chapter, we want to explore with you the tax ramifications (rules and forms, etc.) of eligible foreign entities electing LLC status in the U.S. As the world becomes more reciprocal-trade oriented, we should expect more unincorporated foreign interests seeking entrepreneurial opportunities in the U.S. The U.S. is probably the most lucrative open market in the world. Consequently, we want to focus strictly on foreign LLC activities in the U.S. Such entities and their owners face the daunting task of filing U.S. income tax returns and paying U.S. taxes, then, separately, having to deal with their own national tax authorities for avoiding or minimizing any double taxation. Although our emphasis is clearly on the federal treatment of foreign LLCs, we'll express a comment or two about state law treatment thereof.

Same Elective Options Apply

Whether a business arrangement is an entity separate from its owners for federal tax purposes is a matter of federal tax law. This jurisdiction is independent of whether the arrangement is recognized under state law or under foreign law. Therefore, the pertinent applicable federal rule is IRS Regulation § 301.7701-3(b)(2): *Classification of eligible entities that do not file an election; Foreign eligible entities.* Paragraph (i) of this rule reads:

Unless the entity elects otherwise, a foreign eligible entity is—

(A) A partnership if it has two or more members and at least one member does not have limited liability;

(B) An association if all members have limited liability; or

(C) Disregarded as an entity separate from its owner if it has a single owner that does not have limited liability.

Paragraph (ii) of said rule defines limited liability. It reads:

A member of a foreign eligible entity has limited liability if the member has no personal liability for the debts of or claims against the entity by reason of being a member. This determination is based solely on the statute or law pursuant to which the entity is organized.

When organized under foreign law, it is seldom clear as to the extent of personal liability imposed, or whether such liability is limited or not. In most cases, foreign organizational laws are silent on these matters. One reason for this silence is that no other nation in the world is as litigation driven as is the U.S. Furthermore, on matters of business law, the legal interpretation of words and phrases in a law are not universally accepted. Language and customs play a major interpretive role.

Fortunately, the foreign law situation is not as unmanageable as it appears. Any foreign entity doing business in any state of the U.S. must *register* with the Secretary of that state. Once registered as an LLC, the foreign entity must comply with that state's LLC law just like any domestic LLC. Such compliance will require — at least initially — some ongoing professional guidance.

Meanwhile, at the federal level, IRS Form 8832: ***Entity Classification Election***, is applicable. We discussed this form in detail back in Chapter 4. On said form, three checkboxes are intended solely for foreign entities. The captions to these particular checkboxes read:

☐ *A foreign eligible entity electing to be classed as an association taxable as a **corporation**.*

☐ *A foreign eligible entity electing to be classified as a **partnership**.*

☐ *A foreign eligible entity with a single owner electing to be disregarded as a separate entity* [that is, a proprietorship].

Thus, an eligible foreign entity can elect its U.S. tax classification, the same way — on the same form — that a domestic LLC uses. The only obstacle to a foreign entity is knowing the existence of, and gaining access to, Form 8832.

Effective Date & Relevance

Form 8832 is executed upon the affixing of authorized signatures to the Consent Statement to be U.S. taxed as elected. The authorizing signatures are either:

(A) Each member of the electing entity who is an owner at the time the election is filed; OR

(B) Any officer, manager, or member of the electing entity who is authorized (under local law or the entity's organizational documents) to make the election and who represents to having such authorization.

The authorizing agent must also assure the IRS that no *extraordinary transaction* has taken place. Such would occur if 10% or more of foreign ownership interests have been sold, exchanged, or transferred in the U.S. Each such transaction has to be individually traced for tax relevancy reasons.

An eligible entity created or organized under foreign law, whose owner-members are foreign citizens, would unlikely, on its own, know about IRS Form 8832. It is reasonable, therefore, to assume that one or more such members would have made at least some preliminary contact with a U.S. business correspondent. The U.S. person or entity could be authorized to be an on-site manager to get the LLC ball rolling. A U.S. manager does not have to be a member of the foreign LLC. He could be a paid manager with the proper authorizing documents and contract.

At some point, a U.S. manager of a foreign LLC has to establish the "effective date" for commencing business in the U.S. This is line 4 on Form 8832, to wit—

Election is to be effective beginning (month, day, year) (see instructions) ▶ ___/___/___

The instructions point out that the effective date is that which is entered on line 4, or, if no entry is made, the date of filing with the IRS Service Center in Philadelphia, PA. The instructions further state that—

An election . . . can take effect no more than 75 days prior to the date the election is filed, nor can it take effect later than 12 months after the date on which the election is filed.

This "grace period" of 75 days before, or 12 months after, filing Form 8832 should provide ample time to work out initial business arrangements, getting a U.S. Tax ID, and perhaps even setting up a U.S. bank account. During this period, there is the issue of "relevance" to be addressed.

The effective date for U.S. tax compliance purposes is set by events which lead to the first U.S. dollar being obligated to be paid to the foreign entity. This is where Regulation § 301.7701-3(d)1): **Foreign entity relevance**, comes in. The substance of this regulation is that—

A foreign eligible entity's classification is relevant when its classification affects the liability of any person for federal tax or information purposes. [It is that date on which] an event occurs that creates an obligation to file a federal tax return, information return, or statement for which the classification of the entity must be determined.

There is an ideal way to document this "relevant date." Have the U.S. paying source write a check payable to the foreign entity in its LLC name. Have the U.S. manager make a photocopy of this check. Then, using the U.S. Tax ID, set up a U.S. bank account, and deposit that check. Keep the deposit receipt as the date of verification of what took place. This need only be done for the first U.S. income source event. This and other relevant matters are depicted, for instructional summary purposes, in Figure 8.1. A foreign LLC may need to register in more than one U.S. state.

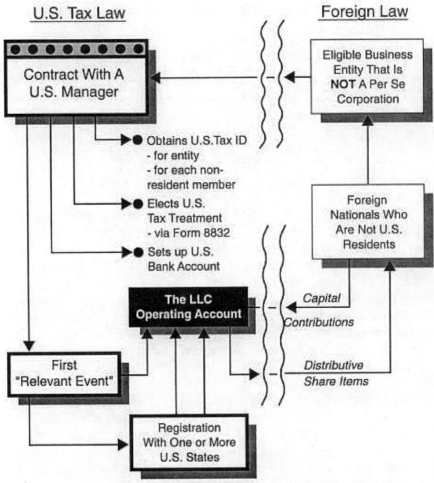

Fig. 8.1 - The "Scheme of Things" With a Foreign LLC in the U.S.

Registering with Each State

All 50 states of the U.S. recognize Form 8832 as evidence of a foreign LLC's federal tax classification. Said form, however, is no substitute for each state's separate law for transacting business within its boundaries. Each state has its own registration procedures. If doing business in more than one U.S. state is intended, registration with each such state is necessary.

Typically, the state-law prerequisites are—

1. Before transacting intrastate business in this state, a foreign limited liability company shall register with the Secretary of State.

2. The laws of the state or foreign country under which a foreign LLC is organized shall govern its organization and internal affairs and the liability and authority of its managers and members.

3. A foreign LLC may not be denied registration by reason of any difference between those laws and the laws of this state.

4. Annexed to the application for registration shall be a certificate from an authorized public official of the foreign LLC's jurisdiction of organization to the effect that the foreign LLC is in good standing in that jurisdiction.

5. In order to register, a foreign LLC shall submit to the Secretary of State application for registering as a foreign LLC, signed by a person with authority to do so under the laws of the state of its organization, on a form prescribed by the Secretary of State [where the business is to be conducted].

[Excerpts from California LLC law, Chapter 10: Foreign Limited Liability Companies; Sections 17450 through 17457.]

In the case of California, there is an officially prescribed Form LLC-5: *Limited Liability Company Application for Registration.* Among other items, the form requires designation of the name under which the foreign LLC proposes to register and transact business, the state or country under whose laws it was formed, its date of formation, an agent within the state for service of process, the principal office in-state, and the type of business intended. When the filing fee is paid and all papers are in order, a Certificate of Registration is issued. Thereafter, the foreign LLC may conduct business, file tax forms and information returns, just like any other domestic LLC. Recall Chapters 2 and 3 in this regard.

The only difference is the cloud of suspicion that could be raised were a domestic LLC to create a foreign-subsidiary LLC, which then would re-register as a foreign entity in the U.S.

Federal Form 1065 Revisited

Back in Chapter 6, we addressed various tax forms and schedules applicable to a domestic multi-member LLC. As pointed out then, the applicable federal form when there are two or more LLC members is Form 1065: *U.S. Return of Partnership Income*. Elsewhere, we pointed out that until the Internal Revenue Code is amended to expressly accommodate limited liability companies, the "partnership model" is to be used. Even with this model, there is no separate form (such as 1065-F) for a foreign partnership. Consequently, whether an LLC or a partnership, domestic or foreign, Form 1065 is entity required.

The only IRS-recognized evidence on Form 1065 that designates it as an LLC return is its Schedule B (on page 2): *Other Information*. At Question 1, there is a checkbox for signifying a domestic LLC and another for signifying a foreign partnership. There is no checkbox preprinted: Foreign LLC. There is, however, a blank checkbox labeled: *Other* ▶ ☐_____

The clear intention is that one check the box at the blank line, then enter: *Foreign limited liability company*. Rather than using the letters "LLC," we suggest spelling out the whole term.

In addition to the above, there are 11 other questions on Schedule B (1065). They are checkbox answerable "Yes" or No". Some are self-explanatory; some are not applicable. Others require some explanation on our part. When reading any of the questions, you have to mentally translate the word "partner" into "LLC member," and word "partnership" into "LLC entity."

For example, Question 3 as translated reads:

Did the partnership [LLC entity] *own any interest in another partnership* [LLC entity] *or in any foreign entity that was disregarded as an entity separate from its owner under Regulations . . .?*   ☐ *Yes* ☐ *No*

While answering this question may be straightforward, the reason for asking it may not be apparent. The IRS concern is the potential for "switching money" between entities (from U.S. based foreign LLCs to foreign based entities and LLCs) in an endeavor to avoid U.S. income tax. There is nothing inherently wrong with transferring money and property overseas so long as the rules for *Withholding of Tax on Nonresident Aliens and Foreign Corporations* are followed [IRC Sections 1441 through 1446].

A more direct inquiry pertaining to money and property transfers overseas is Question 6. It reads quite simply—

> *Does this partnership* [LLC entity] *have any foreign partners* [LLC members]?　　　　　　　　　　　□ *Yes* □ *No*

Surely, a foreign LLC would have foreign members: some or all as individuals, or some or all as entities. When answering "Yes" to this question, the IRS computer searches for compliance with the "withholding of tax" rules referenced above. We'll expand on these rules later. In the meantime, we present Figure 8.2 as means for focusing on the importance of Schedule B (Form 1065) for foreign entity LLCs. The purpose of its focus question is to assess the true economic effectiveness of the LLC versus that of an abusive tax shelter.

Foreign Accounts Question

We are continuing with Schedule B (1065). The last of the questions are 9, 10, 11, and 12. All are directed at foreign financial accounts, foreign trusts, foreign business entities, and foreign correspondents. Most surely, a U.S. based foreign LLC would have one or more types of financial arrangements with its foreign owners and investors. As nonresidents of the U.S., they have their own local bank accounts and regional financial institutions . . . which they obviously prefer.

Instead of citing the questions in the "partnership language" in which they are printed on Schedule B (1065), we'll paraphrase them as though they were written expressly for LLCs. In this vein, Question 9 reads:

> *Did the LLC have an interest in or a signature or other authority over a financial account in a foreign country?* □ *Yes* □ *No. If "Yes," enter name of country and see filing requirements for Form TD F 90-22.1* ▶ _____

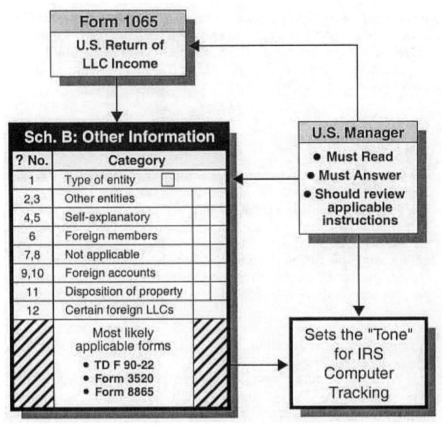

Fig. 8.2 - Categorizing the 12 "Must Answer" Questions on Sch. B (1065)

Form TD F 90-22.1 is **not** an IRS form. It is a Treasury Department form (hence the "TD"; the "F" is "foreign"); when completed, it is mailed directly to the Department of Treasury at the address preprinted on the lower portion of each page of the form. Form TD F 90-22.1 is required only if the aggregate value in all accounts in foreign countries exceeds U.S. $10,000. The form is titled: ***Report of Foreign Bank and Financial Accounts***. It asks for the number of foreign accounts, the type and maximum value of each (by checkboxes), each account number, the name of each account owner, the name of the foreign bank or financial institution, and the country where each account is held.

Question 10 on Schedule B (1065) reads:

Did the LLC receive a distribution from, or was it the grantor of, or transferor to, a foreign trust? □ *Yes* □ *No. If "Yes," see instructions for the filing of Form 3520.*

Form 3520 is an IRS form and is titled: ***Annual Return to Report Transactions with Foreign Trusts and Receipt of Certain Foreign Gifts.*** This is a very formidable form. It consists of 6 pages of tax and financial information and is supplemented by 12 pages of instructional text. If your LLC transfers any money to a foreign **trust** or receives a distribution from one, filing is required. The form is not intended for ordinary business transactions between the LLC entity in the U.S. and its owner-members resident in foreign countries. Transactions with foreign trusts are an entirely different matter. They *imply* — and often are — motivated by tax avoidance reasons only.

Question 11 reads:

Was there a distribution of property or a transfer (by sale or death) of an LLC interest? □ *Yes* □ *No. If "Yes," the LLC may elect to adjust the basis of the LLC assets under Section 754* [re adjustment to basis].

When there is a transfer of LLC ownership interests by sale or death, the new acquirer of those interests will have a higher relative percentage of ownership than the continuing members. This arises because, more often, the transfer(s) take place at higher market valuations than the contributing value by the transferor. This puts the continuing members at a disadvantage, relatively, until the basis of the LLC assets are readjusted. IRC Section 754: ***Manner of Electing Optional Adjustment to Basis of*** [LLC] ***Property***, and its regulations, address what otherwise could produce an inequity in ownership interests.

Question 12 reads:

Enter the number of Forms 8865 attached to this return ▶ ____

Another form? What is it? The answer is extremely important where a foreign LLC is involved.

The Cross Hairs of Form 8865

Form 8865 is titled: *Return of U.S. Persons with Respect to Certain Foreign Partnerships* [LLCs]. This is truly a formidable tax return: 7 tax pages plus 27 pages of instructions. Among other items, the instructions define what is meant by a "U.S. Person" and the term "Certain." From our previous comments, you should be aware by now that the word "Partnership" translates directly into "Limited Liability Company" or LLC. As a result, foreign LLCs are directly in the cross hairs of Form 8865.

The term "U.S. person" means—

A citizen or resident of the U.S., a domestic LLC, a domestic corporation, and any estate or trust that is not foreign.

This is a broad swath of potential filers of the subject form. The term "resident" includes a foreign citizen residing in the U.S. under the: *Substantial presence test* of Section 7701(b)(3)(A) [exceeding 183 days for current and two preceding years].

The word "certain" in the title of Form 8865 refers to one of four categories of filers. A thumbnail description of each of these categories is—

Category 1 — A U.S. person owning, directly or indirectly, more than 50% interest in the foreign LLC.

Category 2 — A U.S. person owning 10% or greater interest in a foreign LLC controlled by U.S. persons each owning at least 10% interests.

Category 3 — A U.S. person contributing property to a foreign LLC in exchange for at least a 10% ownership interest therein, or whose value of property contributed exceeds $100,000.

Category 4 — A U.S. person incurring a *reportable event* with respect to a foreign LLC; such an event is either an acquisition, disposition, or change of ownership interests referenced to the "at least 10%" filing threshold.

In view of the potential ownership interests above, it is difficult to visualize a U.S. manager of a foreign LLC not having some ownership interest in the foreign entity which he manages on-site. If not directly himself, then indirectly through family members and close business associates.

Schedule K-1: 1065 vs. 8865

This may be a bit of trivia, but note the last two digits of 10**65** and 88**65**. The two digits "65" signify a partnership return or, in our case a federal LLC return. Many income-taxing states use these same two digits to signify their partnership returns. For example, California uses Form 5**65** for its partnerships. The purpose for states' doing so is to better coordinate the transfer of tax information between federal and state authorities for the same class of returns being filed.

We now tell you that Schedule K-1 (1065) and Schedule K-1 (8865) have identical titles: *Partner's* [LLC Member's] *Share of Income, Deductions, Credits, etc.* Except for information differences just below the two headings, the distributive share items are identical: line-by-line, category-by-category. In fact, the instructions to Schedule K-1 (8865) say—

If more guidance is needed to complete Schedules K and K-1 of Form 8865, refer to the Form 1065 instructions.

The information portion of K-1 (8865) requires designation of the following percentages of interest in a foreign LLC:

	Start of Year	End of Year
Capital	-------------- %	-------------- %
Profits	-------------- %	-------------- %
Deductions	-------------- %	-------------- %
Losses	-------------- %	-------------- %

The 10% threshold for filing Form 8865 is that percentage which exists "at any time" during the taxable year of the foreign LLC. This 10% pertains to—

THE PROS & CONS OF LLCs

*An interest equal to 10% of the capital interest, an interest equal to 10% of the profits interest, **or** an interest to which 10% of the deductions or losses are allocated. For purposes of determining a 10% interest, the **constructive ownership** rules [re proportionality] shall apply.*

There are two constructive ownership rules. Rule 1 pertains to entities, whereas Rule 2 pertains to individuals. Rule 1 addresses the proportionality of owners in that—

*An interest owned **directly or indirectly by or for** a corporation, partnership [LLC], estate, or trust shall be considered as being owned proportionately by its owners.*

Rule 2 states that—

*An individual is considered to own an interest owned **directly or indirectly by or for** his family. The family of an individual incudes only that individual's spouse, brothers, sisters, ancestors, and lineal descendants.*

The constructive ownership rules are an antidote to tax-perceived evasive transactions. Such transactions are those arranged solely for the purpose of diluting ownership interests to below 10% so as to avoid any filing of Form 8865. The antidote rules are predicated upon the "economic influence" doctrine. That is, a U.S. person in an influential position may actually control 54% of a foreign LLC with only an ostensible 9% direct interest. Indirectly, he may influence five members of his close circle of family and friends, each of whom owns a 9% interest [9% + (5 x 9%) = 54%]. Tax evasive transactions are more prevalent where there are U.S. interests in foreign LLCs, foreign trusts, and foreign financial accounts. There is widespread misperception that U.S. money outside of the U.S. is "unreachable" by the IRS. Nothing could be farther from the truth.

Aliens: Resident vs. Nonresident

An alien is a foreign born person who has not acquired U.S. citizenship. For U.S. tax purposes, there are two classes of aliens:

resident and nonresident. Alien individuals resident in the U.S. are taxed on their worldwide income at graduated rates, the same as U.S. citizens. Nonresident aliens are taxed the same as U.S. citizens only to the extent that their income is "effectively connected" with the active conduct of a trade or business in the U.S. Otherwise, a flat rate of 30% (or lower treaty rate) applies to "fixed or determinable" income that derives from U.S. sources which are not effectively connected with a U.S. trade or business.

The terms "resident" and "nonresident" are defined in the 2,400 statutory words of Section 7701(b): *Definition of Resident Alien and Nonresident Alien*. A resident alien is one who—

(i)   has been lawfully admitted for permanent residence in the U.S. as an immigrant in accordance with the "green card" immigration laws; or

(ii)   meets the substantial presence test of more than 183 days over a 3-year "formula period"; or

(iii)   after 31 days of consecutive physical presence in the U.S. during his first year, who voluntarily elects to become a resident for tax purposes only: not for immigration purposes.

A nonresident alien is one who is neither a citizen of the U.S. nor a resident of the U.S. Residency rules are relaxed for travelers, teachers, medical care, foreign officials, etc. The tax treatment of a nonresident depends on the above-mentioned source-of-income doctrines: (a) effectively connected, and (b) fixed and determinable. That income which is not effectively connected with a trade or business within the U.S. is deemed to be "fixed or determinable," either periodically or annually.   Fixed or determinable income is that which is characterized as interest, dividends, rents, royalties, pensions, annuities, salaries, wages, remuneration, and capital gains and losses on corporate stock held for investment purposes.

The term "effectively connected" income is that which derives strictly from the active conduct of a trade or business within the U.S., which potentially adds U.S. jobs. The factors taken into account shall include whether—

*(A) the income, gain, or loss is derived from assets **used in** or **held for use in** the conduct of such trade or business, or*

*(B) the activities of such trade or business were **a material factor** in the realization of the income, gain, or loss* [IRC Sec. 864(c)(2)].

A foreign LLC doing business in the U.S. via a U.S. resident manager is clearly an effectively connected trade or business. Thus, also, is the distributive share of income, gain, or loss that passes through to the nonresident member-owners of the LLC. The "effectively connected" automatically triggers withholdings.

Withholding at Source

Nonresident aliens and foreign corporations who are members of a U.S. managed foreign LLC are subject to draconian withholding-at-source rules. We say "draconian" because the withholdings are at the highest tax rates permissible under U.S. law; the rates are applied to the highest possible effectively connected taxable income; and the withholdings are treated as "deemed distributions of basis" until U.S. nonresident income tax returns are filed by an LLC member. Whenever an ownership interest is sold or otherwise transferred, after there has been a deemed distribution of basis, maximum capital gains result . . . and maximum withholdings occur. The preemptive mandate for these rules is IRC Section 1446.

Section 1446 is titled: ***Withholding Tax on Amounts Paid by Partnerships to Foreign Partners***. As always with federal LLC matters, the word "partners'" has to be read as "LLC members'." The thrust of Section 1446 is that a foreign LLC conducting business in the U.S. is treated as a corporation for tax computation and withholding purposes. This means that an entity-level tax is imposed, withheld, and paid over (to the U.S. Treasury) before there is any pass-through of distributive share items to individual members. For an understanding of the concept we are describing, we present Figure 8.3. The withholding applies also to the gross proceeds derived from the disposition of real property in the U.S., by its foreign owners [Section 1445].

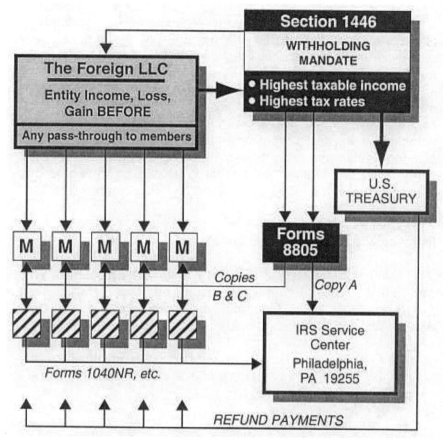

Fig. 8.3 - The Intentional Tax Over-Withholding on Foreign LLC Members

The withholding and payover require special tax forms of their own. This should come as no surprise. There are three such forms, namely:

Form 8804 — *Annual Return for Partnership* [LLC] *Withholding Tax (Section 1446)*

Form 8805 — *Foreign Partner's* [Member's] *Information Statement of Section 1446 Withholding Tax*

Form 8813 — *Partnership* [LLC] *Withholding Tax Payment Voucher (Section 1446)*

These forms are prepared by the Withholding Agent: the U.S. manager of the foreign LLC. When completed, the forms are sent separately to the IRS Service Center in Philadelphia, PA. They are **not** attached to Form 1065 (the "Return of Income") for the LLC.

It is Form 8805 that is significant for each LLC foreign member. It indicates not only the type of member: individual, corporation, other; it also shows in abbreviated manner how the withholding tax was computed. Because of the off-the-top way of computing the maximum-possible taxable income at the LLC entity level, the withholding amount is guaranteed to exceed that which would actually be due, when and if a nonresident U.S. income tax return is filed.

Nonresident Returns: Form 1040NR

Two copies of Form 8805 (Withholding Statement) are transmitted to each foreign withholdee. **Copy B** is marked: *Keep for your records*; **Copy C** is marked: *Attach to your Federal tax return.* The very last line on both of these copies says—

Total tax credit allowed to partner [LLC member] *under Section 1446. Claim this amount as a credit against your U.S. income tax on Form 1040NR . . . etc.* ▶ _____

The clear implication is that, if a foreign resident (with effectively connected income from a trade or business within the U.S.) does not file a U.S. tax return, the U.S. Treasury keeps his withheld money. It does so knowing full well that the withheld amount far exceeds the true tax amount. The burden of proof is on the withholdee to come forward and stake his claim for a refund.

Form 1040NR is titled: *U.S. Nonresident Alien Income Tax Return.* The 1040NR applies not only to foreign individuals, it applies also to foreign estates and trusts (who are LLC members). Among the usual items in the headportion of a tax return, the nonresident alien filer is asked:

Of what country were you a citizen or national during the tax year? ▶ _____

*Give address **outside of the U.S.** to which you want any refund check mailed* [after IRS review and approval].

Excluding attachments, Form 1040NR is a 5-page form . . . plus 32 pages of instructions. Pages 1 and 2 are similar in format to the corresponding pages of Form 1040 for citizens and residents of the U.S. Beyond this format similarity, the 1040NR is far more complicated than a 1040. There are three reasons that account for this added complexity:

[A] The income items on page 1 are only those amounts that are "effectively connected" with a U.S. trade or business. This requires a careful reading of the instructions so as to avoid any non-U.S. sources of income.

[B] The income and tax on U.S. sources **not** effectively connected with a U.S. trade or business are itemized separately on page 4. This itemization includes any capital gains or losses from the sale or exchange of property in the U.S.

[C] Page 5: *Other Information*, tries to nail down the filer's citizenship, his passport number, and when entry to, or departure from, the U.S. were made (if any); whether the filer is a dual-status taxpayer; whether the filer is an expatriate; and the filer's total foreign source income not effectively connected with a U.S. trade or business.

A conscientious foreign resident could easily get the impression that Form 1040NR is deliberately designed to discourage its filing. This could be. But there's a dollarized carrot in the *Payments* portion of the form on its page 2. A preprinted line there reads—

U.S. tax withheld at source:

- From other than "effectively connected" sources $_____

- By partnerships [LLCs] under Section 1446 $_____

- On disposition of U.S. real property interests $_____

If there is an excess of these withholdings over the tax computed, the filer is given the choice of receiving a U.S. refund check at his foreign address or authorizing its direct deposit electronically into his U.S. bank account (if he has one).

At this stage in our presentation, we are compelled to make a philosophical observation. From the point of view of free trade and globalization of the world, the filing of U.S. nonresident income tax returns conveys a superb subliminal message. Such returns, we think, influence the greater use of the U.S. dollar as an international currency, and the greater use of English as an international language. No other tax system in the world is as intrusive into the financial affairs of individuals — whether domestic or foreign — as is the Internal Revenue Code.

There is also a corollary to this observation. It derives from the advent of the Internet worldwide mixed with the advent of LLCs worldwide. The mix of these two advents fosters, on one hand, the enhanced world marketing of goods and services. On the other hand, unfortunately, there's a more sinister side. The volatile Internet-LLC mix opens up unimaginable opportunities for tax and financial fraud . . . also worldwide! Concerned about this, we cite in the next chapter specific examples of how LLCs in cyberspace can go wild.

9

CON ARTISTRY INDICATORS

The Flexible Economic Features Of A Multi-Member (Partnership) LLC Comprise The Very Magnet For Its Breakdown. Such An LLC Can Become The Target Of Con Artists Who Engage In Financial Manipulation, Contractual Intrigue, And Outright Tax Evasion Schemes. The Result Can Be Losses of Members' Capital To As High As $1 Billion ($1,000,000,000). We Cite A "Master Con" [MDL-731] Illustrative Example. Most Artistry Of Abuses In Current Judicial Records Arises From Limited Partnerships. We Regard Such Cases As a Prelude To Expectations With LLCs. Also Expect "Nonrecourse Financing" By LLC Members.

There are many features that make multi-member LLCs attractive for unincorporated business activities. Foremost is the universal and euphoric — and not well understood — attraction of the limited liability doctrine. As a special entity of its own, an LLC can act organizationally like a C-type corporation. There is no limit to the number of members that can be invited on board. There is no limit to the type of members, be they individuals, trusts, other LLCs, partnerships, corporations, exempt entities (such as charitable institutions and retirement plans), foreign persons, or foreign entities. There is no limit to the number and types of legal businesses that can be engaged in, when not otherwise prohibited by law (federal or state). And, best of all, there is no limit to the amount of "whisper type" (word of mouth) capitalization that can be amassed into the LLC treasury.

Unfortunately, these are the very features that make an LLC a wide open, wild west attraction for con artists. An LLC is like a powerful magnet. It draws in those who are cunning enough to beat the odds and walk away with tons of money, pay no tax, leave no trail, and avoid responsibility for damages they have done to others. Their tunnel focus on the letters "LL" (Limited Liability) enables them to be conscience free of any restitutional obligations.

Con artists are masters of glib persuasion. They are perceived to be persons of wealth and power; they tend to be arrogant and intimidating. Rather than using their true birth name, they use an alias (assumed name) or the name of an alter-ego entity. They have it all . . . and they want it all . . . including yours.

Accordingly, in this chapter, we want to give you some example indicators how con artists can work their magic. They can work magic on you, and on your associates who are inattentive to business financials. For this showing, we have extracted various scamming schemes from actual tax and court cases. Such schemes, being low-profile, white-collar rip offs are not well publicized. Not many tax professionals know of them either. In every case that we present, somebody has been damaged financially. Will you be next, or will you be alert?

A Common, Ordinary Example

Professional scamming schemes are sophisticated, convoluted, and extremely clever. Rarely is the object of surprise self-evident. You have to look for little clues that, on the surface, are quite innocent but just don't make sense. You ask yourself: "Is this happenstance, or is it intentional? If intentional, who will benefit the most; who will lose the most?

To help you warm up your sense of keenness, consider that you are one of 35 members of an LLC. Several years ago, the LLC bought a warehouse building in an active industrial area. Surrounding property there was appreciating in value. One particular member — we'll call him "Mike" — began pushing to sell the property. He persuaded the management team to do so. Mike provided professional market data to convince management to set the selling price at $1,000,000 ($1 million). After taking into account the LLC's adjusted basis in the property and its selling expenses, Mike computed that the capital gain would be around $600,000. He wanted the lion's share of that gain.

Just 10 days before the sale, Mike plunked down $100,000 cash as additional contribution to his capital account in the LLC. As of the date of sale, he had a 50% economic interest therein. Just 10 days after the sale, Mike withdrew his $100,000 and demanded $300,000 of the capital gain as his "distributive share" of the proceeds. [$600,000 x 50% = $300,000.]

Come on, now: $300,000 for a 20-day voluntary loan to the LLC. How unreasonable can one be? To a con artist, reasonableness is not a feature of his temperament.

If Mike's demand is not met, he gets angry and threatens to get a high-powered attorney to tear apart the LLC operating agreement. He already knows that the agreement has no prohibition whatsoever against his 20-day incursion strategy. He knows this because it was *he* who diverted attention from any such provision in the agreement.

Let us illustrate how egregious and unreasonable Mike is. Suppose that the warehouse property was held by the LLC for 1,000 days before it was sold. The true percentage of Mike's enhanced participation in the property holding would be 10 days divided by 1,000 days, or 1%. Mike gets no transaction credit for his remaining in the LLC for 10 days after the property was sold. Thus, instead of the $300,000 he demanded, he would be entitled to just 1% of the $600,000 gain or $6,000.

A $6,000 return on a $100,000 "investment" for 10 days is the equivalent of a 219% annual rate of gain. ($6,000/100,000 x 365 days/10 = 2.19 or 219%.) Would Mike accept this fair share in an honorable manner?

Absolutely not! He has already directed his attorney to petition the applicable state court to freeze all distributions from the LLC until he has had a "fair trial." At this point, other members panic and, what was once a successful LLC, falls apart.

A "Master Con" Setup

The foregoing example of con artistry is the simplest of all forms. It is a "unitary con" — a single operator going after a few thousand dollars from a few unsuspecting investors. A "master con" works with "associate cons" to pull off some really big deals, literally *billions* of dollars. The case we have in mind is synopsized as *MDL-731 — Tax Refund Litigation v. U.S.,* CA 2, 93-1 USTC ¶ 50,173 989 F2d 1290. The published case consists of approximately 10,860 words of judicial text. The master con was Irving Cohen (we'll refer to him as "Irving") and four associate cons, either as persons or as entities.

The record is vague as to Irving's educational background. It is clear, though, that he's had extensive legal training and was steeped in business and contract law. He probably was an attorney. He formed three corporations: Madison, Inc. and two subsidiaries: Townsend, Ltd. and Universal, Ltd. He was the President and CEO of each corporation. All three were formed in Las Vegas, Nevada for approximately $6,000 in registration fees and costs. After formation, all shares in the corporations were immediately transferred into an irrevocable trust for the benefit of Irving's several children.

Townsend, Ltd., intended as a leasing entity, subsequently created 35 separate limited partnerships. Similarly, Universal, Ltd., intended as a publishing entity, established 60 limited partnerships. (Read "limited partnership" as comparable to an LLC.) The 95 limited partnerships were pure paper creations by Irving to attract sophisticated investors into publishing ventures (books and software) for which certain tax credits and tax deductions could be claimed on their personal income tax returns. In other words, Irving was selling tax benefits. He was not offering any potential of profit sharing. He was selling tax writeoffs disproportionate (2 or more times) to the amount of cash on the line. How did he proceed to do this?

Irving induced four of his associates in New York to form a general partnership: Barrister Equipment Associates. The Barrister function was to act as a general partner for each of Irving's 95 limited partnerships. Barrister then engaged Chadwick Investment Co., an S corporation in New York, to market the partnership units (read as LLC units) to qualified investors. Irving set the sales price of each unit at from $100,000 to $1,000,000 ($1 million) depending on each investor's "comfort level." All investors had to sign an "acceptance agreement" (prepared by Irving) that each one's net worth was greater than $1,000,000.

> *Editorial Note*: It is a fairly well established securities solicitation principle that, when one's net worth (assets minus liabilities) exceeds one million dollars, that person is a sophisticated investor. Should such a person lose his entire investment, he has no legal recourse. He should have known better or, at least, should have investigated more thoroughly before investing.

At the end of a two-year marketing period, a total of 3,774 individual investors had joined the tax sheltering frenzy. That's 3 thousand, 7 hundred, 74 persons. A grand total of $2,000,000,000 ($2 *billion*) was raised. Of this amount, $1.92 billion or 96% went directly into Irving's children's trust!

How the Irving Scheme Worked

The best that we can figure out, the scheme worked like this. Madison, Inc. (Irving) was to purchase certain properties (metallic plates, lithographic film, unencrypted computer discs, and other related equipment) and lease the properties to Townsend and Universal, who in turn were to engage various publishers (formed by Irving) to produce books and software marketable to the general public. Acquisition contracts, leasing contracts, and publishing contracts were all prepared by Irving. No tangible property of any kind was ever acquired, leased, or produced. The entire arrangement was a paper scam.

Of the $2,000,000,000 collected from willing investors, Irving paid out $59,782,312 (59.78 million) in sales commissions and operating expenses to Barrister and Chadwick. This netted Irving and his three corporations (Madison, Townsend, and Universal) the grand sum of $1,940,217,688 ($1.94 billion). From this amount, Irving and his three corporations had to pay to the IRS $13,79,292 ($13.79 million) in penalties for sponsoring abusive tax shelters. The net, net to Irving thus became $1,926,427,396 ($1.92+ *billion*). Since his children's trust held all the stock in Irving's three corporations, all said 1.92+ billion dollars passed directly into that trust!

Not a bad return for two years of con artistry, would you not agree? Irving not only avoided tax, he also avoided jail time.

A "master" of any trade is a master of all in that same trade. As to Irving's four associated cons, they had to pay to the IRS a total of $2,000,740 ($2+ million) in penalties. Even so, they netted $57,781,572 (59,782,312 – 2,000,740) in commissions and expenses. A 57+ million dollar take for two years of "paper pushing" is still an after-penalty profitable arrangement.

The same techniques used by Irving with limited partnership interests, can be — will be — are being — used in LLC arrangements, large and small. Limited partnerships simply predated today's fascination with LLCs. IRC Section 761(a): **Terms Defined; Partnership**, makes the substitution of LLCs quite clear. This subsection reads in part:

> The term "partnership" includes a syndicate, group, pool, joint venture, or **other unincorporated organization** [read as LLC] through or by means of which any business, financial operation, or venture is carried on. [Emphasis added.]

Big Corporation Tax Avoidance

Con artistry is not the exclusive domain of clever individuals. Large corporations get caught up in the intrigue also. For such corporations, the target is not individual investors; the target is the U.S. government itself. Usually, it is the complete avoidance of tax. A published case on point is *AGA Investerings Partnership v. IRS*, 2000-1 USTC ¶ 50,185; 201 F 3d 305. The judicial summary of this case comprises more than 7,000 words.

"ASA Investerings" was a fictional partnership created by Allied Signal, Inc., a well known U.S. corporation. ASA was created by Allied's wholly owned subsidiary, Allied Signal Investment Co. and two foreign private foundations, Barber N.V. and Dominguito N.V. Barber and Dominguito were controlled by the Algemene Bank Netherlands, N.V., a foreign affiliate of Merrill Lynch & Co. of New York, a global brokerage firm. At the time of the ASA creation, Allied Signal was anticipating approximately $550 million ($550,000,000) in capital gain from the sale of its investments in a group of petroleum holdings. The sole purpose of ASA was to convert this gain into a capital loss over a period of several months. Merrill Lynch was the material advisor for this objective and was to be paid a $7,000,000 ($7 million) fee for making all arrangements.

Merrill Lynch advised Allied Signal to use IRC Section 453: *Installment Method of Accounting.* Subsection (b) thereof defines such method as—

A disposition of property where at least 1 payment is to be received after the close of the taxable year in which the disposition occurs.

> *Editorial Note*: As this case unfolds, it is helpful to keep in mind that "Year 1" represents the taxable year of the "disposition event," and that "Year 2," etc. represents the taxable year(s) of the installment payment(s).

With Section 453 as its statutory platform, representatives of Merrill Lynch met with those of Algemene Bank and Allied Signal to work out the details on the Island of Bermuda. Merrill Lynch was to create $850,000,000 ($850 million) in 5-year floating rate notes to be offered by two of Merrill's Japanese bank affiliates. The notes were designated as PPNs (private placement notes) with a LIBOR (**L**ondon **I**nternational **B**ank **O**ffering **R**ate) rate of interest to be paid entirely by Allied Signal. The Algemene Bank (Netherlands) was to make available to the ASA partnership sufficient funds to execute the disposition event (the purchase of Allied's petroleum holdings). In Year 1, Allied was to have a 10% ownership interest in ASA, the other 90% being held by Barber N.V. and Dominguito N.V. In Year 2, Allied was to have a 90% interest in ASA, Barber and Dominguito a 10% interest. In Years 3 through 5 all outstanding PPNs were to be "self-liquidating." They had to be, because there was no established securities market where the PPNs could be traded.

The long and short of the scheme was that in Year 1, ASA realized $550 million in capital gains. Allied Signal recognized 1% of this amount, which was $55 million. The $495 million was foreign capital gains not reportable to the IRS. In Year 2, Allied issued $435 million of its own commercial paper to buy out 80% of the PPNs held by ASA (thus giving Allied a 90% stake in ASA). At this point, Allied held $246 million in PPNs which were subsequently "sold" (to whom it is not clear) for $50 million. The transaction produced a $196 million capital loss for Allied in Year 2. The Year 1, Year 2 effect was that Allied reported to the IRS a

THE PROS & CONS OF LLCs

net, net *capital loss* of $141 million ($55 million gain in Year 1; 196 million loss in Year 2).

Ultimately, the IRS discovered and disallowed the entire scheme. Allied Signal had to recognize the entire $550 million in capital gains. In addition, the approximately $25 million in fees, expenses, and interest paid by Allied also were disallowed as corporate deductions.

Can you not imagine LLCs being entwined into this same kind of misguided venture? An LLC is like a corporation; it is also like a partnership. It can partner with foreign entities and can engage in international money transactions without limit. These are advantages that become disadvantages when misused.

Setup of Bogus LLCs

A September 2005 U.S. Tax Court decision illustrates how easily an LLC can be misused. The case is that of *Hubert Enterprises, Inc. v. IRS*, Dkt No. 16798-03, 125 TC _____. In Hubert, its three corporate officers formed three LLCs, Hubert Subsidiaries, as wholly owned subsidiaries of Hubert Enterprises. Each officer and the corporation became a separate LLC.

The idea was to transfer some $300,000 into the LLCs which, ostensibly, were to acquire various items of machinery and equipment. These acquisitions were to be leased to other companies. As a consequence thereof, each LLC would claim what is called a *Section 179 Expense Election Deduction*. Up to $100,000 per LLC could be expensed this way. The net result was that each Hubert officer as a pass-through LLC member got an equivalent deduction on his/her personal income tax return. This would have been perfectly legal had the transferred funds actually been used for the purposes claimed.

The IRS got in the act when it questioned the disappearance of $300,000 of capital assets on the parent corporation's return. By the time the IRS started its questioning, the LLCs "had gone out of business." As it turned out, the LLC property allegedly being leased was several prior years of acquisitions by the corporation. The corporation itself had already written off the equipment via depreciation deductions. The corporation claimed that the funds advanced to its LLCs were *loans* for the purpose of acquiring its already used equipment. The IRS did not buy this explanation. Subsequently, the matter went to Tax Court.

The U.S. Tax Court concluded as follows—

There was no evidence that supported the corporation's contention that its transfers to the LLC were loans. The transaction was memorialized in a demand note with no fixed maturity date, no written payment schedule, no provision providing periodic payments of principal or interest, no collateral, and no meaningful repayments. . . . Since there was no evidence that the transfers were made with a genuine intention to create a debt, no bad debt deduction is allowed. . . . Moreover, the officers did not invest their own money in the LLC, but transferred money from the corporation that they controlled. Thus, the primary purpose of the transfers was not to benefit the corporation, but its officers.

What was the practical result of the $300,000 transfer arrangement? What bona fide business purpose did it serve?

The transfers to each Hubert officer's LLC were fraudulent. They served no purpose other than to transfer money out of the corporation where it was subject to tax, either as compensation to the officers or as dividends to them. In the LLCs, the Section 179 expense election deduction passed through to the individual officers resulting in no tax to them. Thus, the LLCs were nothing but bogus entities for tax evasion purposes.

Money Laundering Made Simple

Here's an example of how a true business purpose LLC can be corrupted (unwittingly) by a careful money laundering financial lender. Joe and John were each licensed general contractors. They formed their own LLC, Remod Contractors, for remodeling, improving, and repairing residential properties. The two wives helped in the business by taking care of the books, ordering materials, and paying vendors and laborers.

In the early stages of operation, the business was financed by equity loans on Joe's and John's homes. As they took on larger and larger remodeling projects, they encountered increasing difficulties self-financing them. Petty soon, they reached the point of debt saturation. Their bank would not lend them money any more, and their customers were unwilling to prepay, or pay at all, until a job was essentially complete. Joe and John were at a point where the prospects for growing the business had stalled.

Although various friends and relatives were contacted to join the LLC, none did. However, word of Joe's and John's financial needs got around. One day, a referred stranger (whom we'll call Robert) appeared on the scene. He offered Joe and John virtually unlimited money to pursue their construction project. There was just one catch. The money would be loaned in cold cash, in various green paper denominations. The rate of interest would be 1% per month, with repayment due via bona fide bank loans taken out on finished or semi-finished projects.

The cash advances came in handy for paying suppliers, vendors, day laborers, and others in the building trades who prefer cash. Any cash not consumed in the business was deposited in Joe's and John's LLC bank account. The cash deposits generally ran between $3,000 and $7,000 each. When made, the cash deposits were intermixed with other business checks received. All LLC deposits were made irregularly.

One day, John's wife went to the LLC bank to deposit $15,860 in cash. The money was bundled into $100 bills, $50 bills, and $20 bills. The bank teller called the supervisor over to witness the counting of the cash. When the $15,860 amount was confirmed, the supervisor said (to John's wife): "One moment, please." The supervisor phoned the branch manager who came to the teller's window. John's wife was naturally curious about this.

Puzzlement & Surprise: Form 8300

The branch manager said to John's wife: "I'm sorry, ma'm, we can't accept this amount of cash without your filling out this IRS form 8300." Puzzlement, surprise, and queries were exchanged back and forth. The branch manager ended the exchange by pointing to the penalty information in the instructions to Form 8300. The penalties can run from a low of $25,000 to a high of $250,000 for failure to complete the form truthfully: "Under penalties of perjury."

Form 8300 is titled: *Report of Cash Payments over $10,000 Received in a Trade or Business*. The form seeks such information as—

I — Individual from Whom the Cash was Received,

II — Person on Whose Behalf the Transaction Was Conducted,

III — Description of Transaction and Method of Payment, and

IV — Name and Type of Business that Received the Cash.

The form provides 45 entry spaces and 15 checkboxes for furnishing the information requested. It is to be completed within 15 days and sent to the IRS address in the instructions. The bank recipient of the cash wanted a completed copy of Form 8300 for its own records re the source of cash.

When John's wife confronted Robert with the form, he suddenly remembered he had a business appointment elsewhere. He took off, saying he'd be back later. He never showed again. The frequent cash loans immediately ceased.

"What happened?" Joe and John asked each other. John's wife had to struggle with Form 8300 the best she could, with Robert in absentia. It soon dawned on all three that "Robert" was not the real name of the cash lender. He always managed to avoid giving his full name, address, phone number, and social security or other Tax ID number.

Then, one day, a person claiming to be a friend of Robert's showed up. The friend, with a gun conspicuously holstered to his waist, presented a handwritten note addressed to Joe and John. The note demanded that a bank cashier's check in the amount of $15,860 be handed over.

Joe and John then realized that they had been unwittingly drawn into a money laundering scheme. The cash quite evidently came from illegal and under-the-table sources. The withdraws from Joe and John's LLC bank were always in cashier's checks showing no named payer. By the time the $15,860 loan repayment was made, Joe's and John's LLC business had progressed to the point where they could borrow directly from the bank themselves. No further outside cash infusions were needed.

Nonrecourse Financing

In the Joe and John example above, they were the ones ultimately liable for full repayment of the loan. But there can be, and are, situations where no one is ultimately liable. The lender is left with a loss that the borrower claims as a tax loss for himself. The technique uses unsecured promissory notes that the IRS calls: *nonrecourse financing*. A landmark case on point is that of *M.W. Melvin*, CA-9, 90-1 USTC ¶ 50.052.

Taxpayer Melvin was one of 73 limited partners who pledged (prorata) "deferred capital contributions" as collateral for a $3,500,000 (3.5. million) recourse bank loan. Under this arrangement, Melvin's prorata share was 0.6232% or $21,812. Subsequently, $9,000,000 (9 million) was nonrecourse financed through a group of unrelated and unsuspecting private investors who were promised great returns. Instead of great returns, there were great losses: $12,515,318 (12.5 million) to be more precise. Melvin claimed a deductible loss of $78,000 ($12,515,318 x 0.006232) on his tax return. The IRS disallowed the $78,000 but did allow the $21,812 for which he was recourse at-risk.

What happened to the $9,000,000 of nonrecourse money that was lost? The *Melvin* court did not address this specific issue. In reality, the private investors lost the entire $9,000,000 via 73 (recourse worthless) I.O.U.s.

We don't know exactly what happened. Yet, typically, nonrecourse financing goes something like this. In exchange for money, a cooperative lender is given an official-looking document (on high-grade embossed paper) with conspicuously displayed seals, stamps, and signatures. The document is bold-print captioned: PROMISSORY NOTE. On its face, the note indicates the amount borrowed, the high rate of interest to be paid , and the due date for full payment. Prefatory wording indicates that the note is either collateralized, guaranteed, warranted, pledged, accredited, licensed, insured, or some other endearing term implying safety and security.

Often the "security" is some microfractional interest — such as 0.012973 percent — in a high-sounding business operation (located out of state), or in some parcel of realty in a wilderness area or open space preserve, or in items if high-tech equipment and merchandise in a bonded warehouse, or in "proven reserves" in an offshore tax haven. With such a stream of clever and emotionally appealing wording, even the most cynical lender feels confident that he will get his money back. The first indication that he won't get his money back is when the borrowing activity either files for bankruptcy or disappears entirely into thin air. When the lenders realize that they have been taken it is far too late.

Example of "Circular" Financing

We never cease to be amazed by the deceptive brilliance of some entrepreneurs when structuring their financial transactions. It's scary. It is scary because some LLC enthusiasts will want to raise the finessing bar even higher. A good example of what we are getting at is the case of *R.L. Whitmire*, CA-9; 99-1 USTC ¶ 50,563. This is a published case consisting of over 4,000 words of citable judicial inquiry and rationalization. The appeals court itself marveled at the artful structuring of so many layers of protection that precluded any realistic possibility of Whitmire ever being held personally responsible for the repaying of borrowed funds.

Whitmire executed a Subscription Agreement with Petunia, et al, in exchange for a limited partnership interest. He contributed $25,031.50 ($16,281.50 in cash and a recourse promissory note for $8,750) in a double, triple-leaseback computer equipment arrangement. Whitmire also subscribed to his being personally liable under a Petunia-Venture Note for an amount up to 434.75% of his capital contribution. This meant (to Whitmire) that his potential tax deduction could be $108,824.45 ($25,031.50 x 4.3475) for an out-of-pocket cash amount of $16,281.50. If allowed, his deduction would be 6.6837 times his true economic risk. This is a clear tax earmark of a scam.

> *Editorial Note*: The first indicator of a sophisticated scam is the absence of simple round numbers. Trying to mentally absorb and track odd-dollar amounts and uneven fractions and percentages catapults the reader into an early-on state of confusion.

The "Petunia-Venture Note" was the creation of Alanthus Computer Corporation (ACC) which purchased several hundred million dollars of computer equipment. ACC then leased the equipment to Manufacturers Traders Trust Company (MTT). Afterwards, ACC sold the equipment *and* the lease to the Alanthus Corporation. Alanthus paid for the equipment with a recourse loan from Manufacturers Hanover Leasing Corporation (MHLC) which was secured by the equipment. Alanthus entered into a security agreement with MHLC that stated that MTT would make the lease payments directly to MHLC in satisfaction of the loan. With sleight of hand, Alanthus resold the computer equipment to F/S Computer Corporation, and F/S executed an agreement by which F/S assumed all of Alanthus's rights under the MTT lease. In exchange, F/S also assumed all of Alanthus's obligations under the MHLC loan and agreement. On the same day, F/S sold the equipment and assigned the lease to F.I. Venture, subject to MHLC's and MTT's interests in the equipment. Venture immediately resold the computer equipment and assigned the lease to Petunia. In payment, Petunia gave Venture a Limited Recourse Installment Promissory Note — the "Petunia-Venture Note" — whereby all Petunia partners (including Whitmire) were severally and personally liable for each of the installments of principal.

The Appeals court concluded that—

Whitmire crossed the line by shrouding himself in too much protection to leave any "realistic possibility" that he would suffer a loss. . . . Therefore, we affirm the order of the tax court, and hold that Whitmire is not "at risk" within the meaning of section 465 [Deduction limited to the amount of "real money" economically at risk].

Lest some LLC enthusiast is thinking of trying to outsmart Whitmire above, here's a fact you should know. Whitmire entered into his limited partnership arrangement in June, 1980. The matter was not finalized until May, 1999. That's **19 years** of entanglement with the IRS, the U.S. Tax Court, and the U.S. Appeals Court. Though he claimed nearly $120,000 in tax deductions, they were summarily disallowed. In addition, his penalties, interest, and attorney fees approached $250,000. Whitmire could have saved himself much aggravation had he used IRS Form 6198: *At-Risk Limitations*.

10

PARTNERSHIP LLC RULES

A Partnership Form Of Business Is Most Representative Of An LLC Entity With Multiple Members. As Each Member Is A Part Owner, Along With Other Part Owners, Those Who Are More Aggressive Will Benefit At The Expense Of Others, Unless Specific Rules Are Meticulously Followed. There Are 29 Such Rules Directed At Tax Liability, Capital Accounting, Basis Accounting, Contributions Of Money And Property, Distributions, Transfers Of Interests, And Adjustments To Basis. All Focus On "Leveling The Field" Between Members And On Assuring That Transactional Ventures Will Have "Economic Substance."

When several unincorporated persons associate in a profit-seeking venture, they are automatically construed to be a general partnership. This is one of the default classification rules discussed previously in Chapter 4. If the members understand the significance of this automatic classification, no Form 8832 (Entity Classification Election) is needed. That significance is: There is no "automatic" limited liability protection. It is only when the members consent to federally documenting their state-law formation as an LLC, that Form 8832 is required. Thereafter, for simplicity of designation, the LLC entity can be identified as a *Partnership LLC*.

As we saw in the preceding chapter, the pass-through and prorata sharing features of a partnership LLC create opportunities for abuse. Such opportunities arise because an LLC is a *flexible economic arrangement* for conducting joint business affairs. Flexibility is tolerated as a means for increasing the efficiency of a business. It is not tolerated as a means for tax shifting, debt avoidance, and accounting misdeeds. To deter starting an LLC partnership on the wrong foot, some 29 statutory tax laws are prescribed. They cover the gamut known as Subchapter K: *Partners and Partnerships* of the Internal Revenue Code (IRC).

Accordingly, we want to overview with you IRC Subchapter K, and point out its highlights that could make your LLC experience both pleasant and lucrative. As in any serious business endeavor, dedication, hard work, and self-discipline are essential ingredients. For those who believe that, by being an LLC, a magic wand can be waved and all the arduous tax rules will go away, are in for a surprise. For those who are more realistic, the partnership rules actually make sense. They systematize matters for the orderly conduct of business . . . throughout many years.

Categorizing the 29 Rules

In its present form, IRC Subchapter K: *Partners and Partnerships*, does not mention Limited Liability Companies. As we tried to clarify in Chapter 5, when a two-or-more-member LLC is involved, the return preparer has to check the appropriate "Type of entity" box on Form 1065: *U.S. Return of Partnership Income*. Thereafter, one reads the word "partner" as "LLC member," and the word "partnership" as "limited liability company." For example, Section 701 is titled: *Partners, Not Partnership, Subject to Tax*. One has to read this as: "LLC Members, Not LLC Entity, Subject to Tax." This can make for awkward reading of the partnership rules, unless you acclimate yourself to it. Being an LLC does not invalidate the 50 years (commencing 1956) of partnership tax rules designed to prevent abuses when engaged in uincorporated entrepreneurial activities. An LLC, and all of its members, must toe the tax line, just like everyone else.

With the above comments in mind, the arrangement of Subchapter K is grouped into six categories, as follows:

A — Determination of Tax Liability   }
             Sections 701 through 709 (9 rules)   }

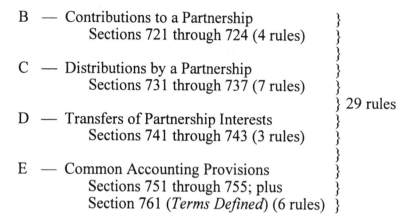

B — Contributions to a Partnership
Sections 721 through 724 (4 rules)

C — Distributions by a Partnership
Sections 731 through 737 (7 rules)

} 29 rules

D — Transfers of Partnership Interests
Sections 741 through 743 (3 rules)

E — Common Accounting Provisions
Sections 751 through 755; plus
Section 761 (*Terms Defined*) (6 rules)

By ordinary counting, 701 through 777, it would appear that there are 77 partnership sections (or rules): not the 29 that we state. There is no discrepancy in what we state. There are "gaps" between the sectional groupings. The gaps permit the inclusion of additional laws as needed. One definite such need is the addressing of LLC partnerships in specific LLC terms. Meanwhile, we eliminate the seven rules (771 through 777) that address Electing Large Partnerships. By definition, a "large partnership" is one having 100 or more members in any given year. In an LLC where each member is an owner-manager, we question the likelihood of an LLC partnership ever becoming this large. Consequently, our rule count is reduced to 29.

In Figure 10.1, we present a complete listing of these 29 rules. We urge that you take a moment and read, line by line, the official titles of these rules. By doing so, you'll get a sense of the seriousness expected of you and your associates, when conducting business as an LLC.

We should tell you that the 29 partnership rules in Figure 10.1 are authorized in some 670 pages of statutory, regulatory, descriptive, and court-brief text. Altogether, approximately 400,000 words are involved. Obviously, in the 24 pages of this chapter, we can only cover selected highlights. Those that we select are directed at those LLC members who seek to be better informed than they presently are through general hearsay and Internet postings. As implied in Figure 10.1, partnership LLC accounting is a process all of its own.

THE PROS & CONS OF LLCs

Section		Rule Title
		INTERNAL REVENUE CODE
		Chapter 1 - Subchapter K - PARTNERS AND PARTNERSHIPS
	A	**Determination of Tax Liability**
701		Partners, Not Partnership, Subject to Tax
702		Income and Credits of Partner
703		Partnership Computations
704		Partner's Distributive Share
705		Determination of Basis of Partner's Interest
706		Taxable Years of Partner and Partnership
707		Transactions Between Partner and Partnership
708		Continuation of Partnership
709		Treatment of Organization and Syndication Fees
	B	**Contributions to a Partnership**
721		Nonrecognition of Gain or Loss on Contribution
722		Basis of Contributing Partner's Interest
723		Basis of Property Contributed to Partnership
724		Character of Gain or Loss on Certain Items
	C	**Distributions by a Partnership**
731		Extent of Gain or Loss on Distribution
732		Basis of Distributed Property Other Than Money
733		Basis of Distributee Partner's Interest
734		Adjustment to Basis of Undistributed Property
735		Gain or Loss on Disposition of Distributed Property
736		Payments to a Retiring or Deceased Partner
737		Precontribution Gain In Certain Distributions
	D	**Transfers of Partnership Interests**
741		Recognition of Gain or Loss on Sale or Exchange
742		Basis of Transferee Partner's Interest
743		Adjustment to Basis of Partnership Property
	E	**Common Accounting Provisions**
751		Unrealized Receivables and Inventory Items
752		Treatment of Certain Liabilities
753		Partner Receiving Income In Respect of Decedent
754		Manner of Electing Optional Adjustments
755		Rules for Allocation of Basis
761		Terms Defined

Fig. 10.1 - Basic Tax Rules For Partners & Partnerships [and LLCs]

The Anti-Abuse Rule

Of the 29 rules listed in Figure 10.1, Section 701 is one of the shortest. It consists of just 35 words. Yet, it is accompanied by nearly 8,000 words of regulations. The most dominant of these regulations (over 7,000 words) is Regulation § 1.701-2: *Anti-abuse rule*. The purpose of this rule is to uphold the for-profit business intent of Section 701 without straying into abusive territory. The implicit intent is to conduct joint business activities (including investments) in a manner that is clearly consistent with all of the income tax provisions of Subchapter K. When valid questions arise, Subchapter K is the official source for answers.

The anti-abuse rule is to assure that three particular Section 701 requirements are met. These are:

1. The partnership must be bona fide and each partnership transaction or series of related transactions . . . must be entered into for a **substantial business purpose.**

2. The form of each partnership transaction must be respected under **substance over form** *principles.*

3. The tax consequences . . . to each partner of partnership operations and of transactions between the partner and the partnership must **accurately reflect** *the partners' [plural] economic agreement and clearly reflect* **each partner's income.** [Emphasis added.]

As a test of whether an LLC partnership meets these requirements, the regulation asks one pointed question:

Was the partnership formed with a principal purpose to reduce substantially the present value of the **partners' aggregate federal tax liability** *in a manner inconsistent with the intent of subchapter K?* [Emphasis added.]

In other words, is the partnership set up primarily as a tax shelter, a tax shifting vehicle among related taxpayers, a tax maneuvering arrangement between offshore (foreign) and onshore (domestic) members, or a trading pool for members with unused losses that otherwise would be tax wasted?

Numerous factors are taken into consideration before the IRS can make a judgment call on the intent question. Most of these factors are synopsized in Figure 10.2. They are condensed directly from Regulation § 1.701-2(c): *Facts and circumstances analysis; factors.* We show seven of such factors.

If the IRS decides that an LLC partnership is primarily tax motivated rather than being business motivated, it can disregard the arrangement in its entirety. The partners are then restored to their individual capacities without any pass-through or prorata sharing benefits whatsoever.

Economic Substance Rule

Section 704 is titled: ***Partner's Distributive Share.*** Its subsections (a) and (b) are titled, respectively: ***Effect of Partnership Agreement*** and ***Determination of Distributive Share.*** The substance of these two subsections is that—

A partner's distributive share of income, gain, loss, deduction, or credit shall . . . be determined by the partnership agreement . . . [OR] in accordance with the partner's [capital] interest in the partnership . . . if the allocation does not have substantial economic effect.

This statutory wording is the economic substance rule for prorata sharing. The "economic substance" — or, substantial economic effect — derives from each member's capital interest (money and property) in the LLC arrangement. The economic benefits and economic burdens from the partnership operations must flow through proportionately to the ownership interests in the venture. If member A's ownership interest is $10,000, for example, and member B has a $30,000 interest, the flow through of benefits and burdens should be (approximately) 25% to member A and 75% to member B [10,000 ÷ 40,000; 30,000 ÷ 40,000]. We say "approximately" because there does not have to be a dollar-for-dollar correlation if the partnership agreement provides otherwise, and other members' interests are not distorted.

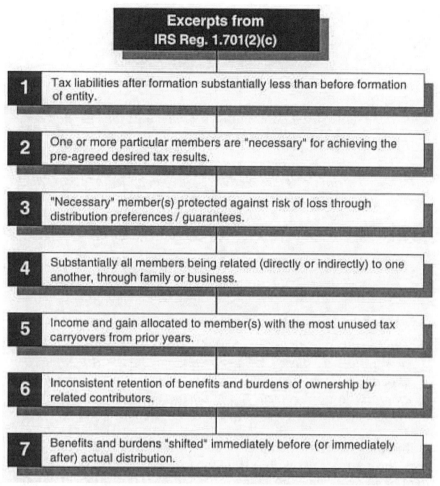

1	Tax liabilities after formation substantially less than before formation of entity.
2	One or more particular members are "necessary" for achieving the pre-agreed desired tax results.
3	"Necessary" member(s) protected against risk of loss through distribution preferences / guarantees.
4	Substantially all members being related (directly or indirectly) to one another, through family or business.
5	Income and gain allocated to member(s) with the most unused tax carryovers from prior years.
6	Inconsistent retention of benefits and burdens of ownership by related contributors.
7	Benefits and burdens "shifted" immediately before (or immediately after) actual distribution.

Excerpts from IRS Reg. 1.701(2)(c)

Fig. 10.2 - Factors Indicative of Tax Motivation Over Business Motivation

The "otherwise", however, must satisfy the *substantial economic effect* test. Why would member A, for example, get only 10% of the benefits, and carry 50% of the burdens? With a 25% ownership interest, member A might agree to accept 20% of the benefits and 30% of the burdens in deference to member B's superior knowledge, contacts, and personal service devotion to the business. How much stretch is there, when trying to achieve substantial economic effect? The "effect" must not distort the economic viability of the entity overall.

The term "substantial economic effect" is defined in Regulation § 1.704-1(b)(2) and its subparagraphs. Pertinent portions read—

*A partner will have economic effect **if, and only if,** throughout the full term of the partnership, the agreement provides—*

> *(1) For determination and maintenance of the partners' [plural] capital accounts,*
>
> *(2) Upon liquidation of . . . any partner's interest, distributions are required to be made in accordance with the **positive capital account balances** of all the partners, . . . after taking into account all capital account adjustments for the partnership, and*
>
> *(3) If such [liquidating] partner has **a deficit balance** in his capital account . . ., he is **unconditionally obligated to restore** the amount of such deficit balance to the partnership.*

*The economic effect of an allocation (or allocations) is substantial if there is a reasonable possibility that the allocation (or allocations) will **substantially affect the dollar amounts** to be received by the partners from the partnership, independent of tax consequences.* [Emphasis added.]

In other words, if member C puts up $10,000 and walks away from the partnership with $100,000 in benefits and no burdens, there is no economic substance. Particularly so if member D puts up $50,000 and gets only $10,000 in benefits while being stuck with $90,000 in burdens. This kind of arrangement is not a bona fide partnership; it is a sham. Member C is a con artist. Such artistry can be prevalent in any joint venture, whether an LLC or not. The intrigue of the letters "LL": *Limited Liability*, can be disarming. Actually, these two letters are quite misleading.

Maintaining Capital Accounts

In principle, all LLC members are treated equally on a per capita basis. This means that if the total capitalization of the partnership is $100,000, for example, the allocation (of income, gain, loss, deduction, or credit) to each partner is proportional to his/her/its capital account balance. For good reason and cause, the partnership agreement may provide for different allocations than the per capita prorations. Nevertheless, it is each partner's capital account balance (at the end of each prescribed accounting period for the partnership) that determines the economic effect on the allocation process.

Therefore, determining and maintaining each partner's capital account (**within** the partnership) is *key* to successful partnership operation. The "determination" aspect thereof turns primarily on the fair market value of property, other than money, that is contributed to the partnership. Money is money, and is valued at whatever denomination is on its face. But valuing property is a different matter altogether. The term "property" includes such variant items as real estate, natural resource interests, machinery, equipment, vehicles, materials and supplies, merchandise inventory, accounts receivable, mortgage notes, promissory notes, private securities, negotiable securities, commodities (gold, wheat, oil), fractional interests in other entities, and so on. Needless to say, market valuing fairly such a wide variety of property items can be a contentious and drawn-out issue. It can become a war zone among serious contributors, con artists, sophisticated schemers, and other money sharks.

For official guidance, we turn to Regulation § 1.704-1(b)(2)(iv)(h): *Determinations of fair market value.* Excerpted portions from this regulation read—

> *The fair market value assigned to property . . . will be regarded as correct,* **provided that** *(1) such value is reasonably agreed to among the partners in arm's-length negotiations, (2) the partners have sufficiently adverse interests . . . and (3) the valuation . . .* [is] *on a property-by-property basis.*

The above relates the determination of a member's *contributions* to his capital account. Maintaining such an account is another matter. The "maintenance" aspect deals with **adjustments** to each account throughout the partnership's operating year. For this aspect, Regulation § 1.704-1(b)(2)(iv)(a):

Maintenance of capital accounts, is instructive. Our position is that this regulation should be mandatory in every LLC operating agreement. This is a statutory requirement: not voluntary.

The pertinent portions of the maintenance regulation read—

*The partners' [plural] capital accounts will be considered to be determined and maintained . . . **if, and only if**, each partner's [singular] capital account is **increased by**—*

> *(1) the amount of money contributed by him to the partnership,*
>
> *(2) the fair market value of property contributed by him, and*
>
> *(3) allocation to him of partnership income and gain (including allocations exempt from tax . . . and adjustments [amortization, depreciation, depletion] to reflect book values)*

*and is **decreased by**—*

> *(4) the amount of money distributed to him by the partnership,*
>
> *(5) the fair market value of property distributed to him,*
>
> *(6) allocation to him of expenditures and liabilities of the partnership, and*
>
> *(7) allocations of any partnership loss and deduction.*

The message above, and in Figure 10.3, is that a lot of capital accounting discipline is required when getting an LLC partnership up and running. Implied in this discipline is that there must be enough capital reserves on hand to meet the liabilities of a partnership LLC, as distinguished from the personal liabilities of each member.

For good capital accounting discipline, keep one point foremost in mind. Each member's capital account within the partnership is NOT his private piggy bank. It is not a cash kitty from which a member may withdraw or borrow money at will. A positive capital balance must be maintained by each member at all times. The moment any member starts behaving cavalierly about his obligation for maintaining a positive balance, that's the time to prepare to cut him loose and terminate his interests in the partnership. Promised restoration of capital deficits are difficult to enforce legally, particularly in an LLC.

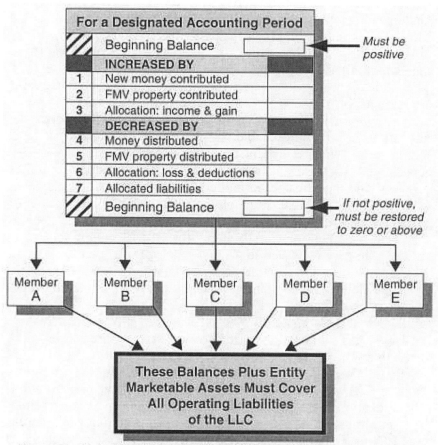

Fig. 10.3 - Mechanics of Members' Capital Accounting for a Solvent LLC

Mandatory Allocation of Debt

Technically, all debt of an LLC partnership is *nonrecourse*. The term "nonrecourse" means that no member can be held personally responsible for repayment of partnership (the entity) debts. Such debts include accounts payable (to suppliers, venders, contractors, etc.), and delinquent payroll, if any. As nonrecourse debts, they lack economic substance. The creditors, lenders, and employees will suffer the economic loss if the partnership does not have sufficient funds to repay its nonrecourse obligations. As a consequence, all LLC arrangements tend to be suspect. Creditors, lenders, and employees worry about getting paid. They want some form of "guarantee" that the LLC partnership will pay them.

The most credible form of guarantee for an LLC is a mandatory allocation of partnership debt to each LLC member. The allocation mandate must be spelled out in the Operating Agreement of the entity. Said agreement is filed with state authorities, where the LLC permit was issued. This makes the allocation legally enforceable, proportionately, upon each LLC member. As we have mentioned previously, an LLC is not — repeat, NOT — an arrangement for defrauding creditors of monies properly due them in the normal course of business. As depicted in Figure 10.4, the LLC situation differs substantially from that of a regular partnership. In a regular partnership, any one general partner can be held personally liable for all partnership debt. He, in turn, can take legal action against other general partners. In an LLC, a creditor or creditors can recover only the per-member allocated debt amount. This means legal action against all LLC members simultaneously, for each's allocated share of the aggregate partnership debt.

How are allocations attributable to nonrecourse debt determined?

Regulation § 1.704-2: *Nonrecourse liabilities*, addresses this point specifically. Unfortunately, it is a 15,000-word regulation. The allocation is based on a *minimum gain chargeback* principle. The "minimum gain" is established (as of a given date) by treating all LLC nonrecourse debt as having been fully discharged for its fair market value. To the extent that this amount exceeds the aggregate marketable assets of the partnership, there is, constructively, minimum gain. This gain is charged back to each LLC member in proportion to his capital interests in the partnership. The chargeback process creates economic substance out of the excess nonrecourse debt. This is because each LLC member now bears his proportionate share of the economic burdens of the enterprise.

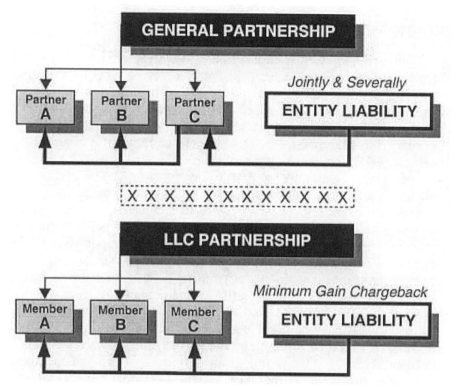

Fig. 10.4 - Liability Comparison Between General & LLC Partnerships

Consider, for example, that the total nonrecourse debt of an LLC partnership is $100,000. The entity assets available for discharging that debt are $80,000. The minimum gain thereby is $20,000. Suppose there were three LLC members with capital interests of 50%, 35%, and 15%. Their respective chargeback amounts would be $10,000; $7,000; and $3,000. These amounts are subtracted from each member's capital account balances (in Figure 7.3). If any negative capital balance occurs, the negative must be restored to at least zero via additional capital contributions from the affected member. IRS regulations allow 90 days in which to restore any negative capital account balance to zero. If this is not done, the partnership is deemed to be abusive, and subject to reallocation of interests. "Reallocation" means that those members with positive account balances before chargeback will not bear any burden of the negative account member(s).

Partnership Accounting Year

Ordinarily, a business entity is permitted to set up its books and records to mirror its "natural business cycle." The idea is to include the full range of ups and downs of income and expenses throughout a 12-month period. This is called the "accounting year" of the business. It can be any 12 months starting January 1st, February 1st, March 1st, . . . December 1st. If starting other than on January 1st, the cycle is a *fiscal year*.

Individuals, generally, must file their income tax returns on a *calendar* year basis. If a partnership files its "return of income" on a fiscal year basis, and its partners file on a calendar year, can you not sense the overlapping of accounting items between the entity and the individuals' returns? There is also opportunity for intentional income deferral by structuring the accounting overlappings. Often, such "structuring" serves no bona fide business purpose other than to satisfy some demanding member.

Suppose, for example, that a partnership's tax year ended on January 31. A calendar-year partner's income allocation from the partnership would be reported by the partner in his tax year ending on December 31. This produces an 11-month deferral of income recognition to the LLC member. If this were deliberately done without regard to IRS tests, it would be disallowed.

To prevent the deferral and distortion of income, gain, loss, deduction, or credit between partners and their partnership, IRC Section 706 applies. This section is titled: ***Taxable Years of Partner and Partnership***. The substance of this 1,300-word mandate is that the LLC partnership must conform its tax year to the tax years of its owners. Three "tests" are used for determining the tax years of the entity owners. These are—

(1) Majority interests: those LLC members having more than 50% ownership of profits and capital.

(2) All principal members: each of whom has at least a 5% interest in the profits and capital.

(3) Least aggregate deferral of income to all members (determined by a quite complex weighting formula).

Our position is that, in an LLC partnership, most owners most likely would be individuals. Hence, the most practical procedure is to adopt a calendar accounting year for the partnership. This simplifies allocation and pass-through matters greatly. Also, it helps to thwart IRS suspicion of using the partnership improperly.

An exception to "our" calendar year rule is provided in subsection 706(b)(1)(C): *Business Purpose*. This subsection reads in part—

> *A partnership may have a* [fiscal] *taxable year . . . if it establishes, to the satisfaction of the* [IRS], *a business purpose therefor. Any deferral of income to its partners shall not be treated as a business purpose.*

To establish a business purpose, the LLC partnership must file Form 1128: *Application to Adopt, Change, or Retain a Tax Year*. This form comprises four full-size pages, over 60 checkboxes, and over 6,000 words of instruction. Take a look at the official form yourself. If you do, you and your LLC associates will be more than anxious to adopt a calendar accounting year for the partnership LLC.

Changes in Members' Interests

LLC members come and go. They want to get in; they want to get out. Some want to increase their capital interests; some want to decrease said interests. Some want to sell or exchange their interests to new members. Some retire; some gift their interests to family members; and some die. What else can you expect of human beings when putting their capital and talents on the line. Still, what effect do these varying ownership interests have on the partnership operation?

Needless to say, all such changes affect the internal accounting of the partnership. Particularly, the allocable sharing aspects. Does a member who enters on October 18th with a $10,000 contribution get a full year's sharing of the distributive items (income, gain, loss, deduction, credit)? Of course not. He gets 75 days' worth of allocation (365 − 290 days from January 1 through October 17). Or, suppose a high-roller member wants out on

January 15th. Does he get a full year's allocation of the shared items? Again, of course not. He gets only 15 days' worth of allocation (January 1 through January 15). In other words, as members come and go, the role of **participant days** takes on an accounting importance of its own.

As per IRC subsection 706(d): ***Determination of Distributive Share When Partner's Interest Changes***, the LLC partnership may use—

> *any method prescribed . . . which takes into account the varying interests of the partners in the partnership during* [its] *taxable year.*

This statutory authority leads to accounting in *dollar days* as well as in *membership days*. Can you not imagine the distributive sharing complexity when members come and go in an undisciplined way?

LLC partnerships particularly attract shrewd and cunning members. Such persons are the type who want everything in their favor. They seek to time their entry into and withdrawal from the partnership just before *and* just after a major partnership transaction takes place. For example, the partnership sells its small shopping center for $1,500,000. After taking into account the partnership's adjusted basis in the property and its selling expenses, the partnership's capital gain is $1,000,000, say. Just 10 days before the sale, a shrewd member plunks down $100,000 as additional contribution to his existing capital. As of the date of sale, he has a 50% ownership interest in the partnership. Just 10 days after the sale, he withdraws his $100,000 and demands $500,000 of the capital gain as his "distributive share" of the proceeds. Come on, now: $500,000 for a 20-day voluntary loan to the partnership. This is arrogance at its very worst.

There is really only one way to handle the above matter and others like it. Limit a member's entry into, and withdrawal from, the LLC partnership to specific accounting-period ending dates: March 31, June 30, or September 30, for example. Furthermore, limit participation in entity transactional gains or losses to the percentage of days a partner participated during the total holding-period days that the property was owned by the partnership.

Let us illustrate. Suppose that in the 20-day incursion example above, the shopping center was held by the partnership for 1,000 days before it was sold. The percentage of incursion participation in the property holding would be 10 days divided by 1,000 days, or 1%. The high roller gets no transaction credit for remaining in the partnership for 10 days after the property was sold. Thus, instead of the $500,000 he demanded, he would be entitled to just 1% or $5,000 only. Does **your** LLC agreement cover situations like this? If not, this and other items should be addressed, as we explain in the next chapter.

Basis & Adjustments Thereto

The term "basis" (as you already know) is a *tax reference* for establishing the amount of gain or loss from a property transaction. One's basis includes his acquisition cost of the property, plus added items of cost while holding the property, minus statutory adjustments, such as depreciation, depletion, etc. Special basis rules apply when property is acquired by gift, inheritance, exchange, or assumption of a prior owner's debt. The basis rules of general application are found in Subchapter O of the Internal Revenue Code: *Gain or Loss on Disposition of Property*. Some 30 such rules (Sections 1011 – 1060) are prescribed. The key one is Section 1011: *Adjusted Basis for Determining Gain or Loss*. All are beyond our discussion here. We reference them only to have you focus on **property dispositions**.

A "property disposition" occurs when an LLC member transfers his ownership interests in a property item to a partnership with others. Immediately before the transfer takes place, the contributing member has a tax basis in that property. If, instead of transferring the property to the partnership, it were sold to a party outside of the partnership, gain or loss would be tax recognized at that time. But when contributing property to a partnership, no immediate gain or loss is tax recognized [Section 721].

Meanwhile, when a member contributes money and property to a partnership, he does so for the express purpose of acquiring (purchasing) an ownership interest therein. Such an interest is a capital asset. Unless the contributor pays all cash, what appears to be an accounting anomaly develops. His tax basis in his ownership interest will differ — often substantially —from his capital basis in the partnership. Here's an example of this "anomaly."

A member buys a $100,000 capital interest in a partnership. To do this, he conveys to the partnership $20,000 in money and property whose fair market value is $80,000. His tax basis in the property is $45,000. This amount includes a $40,000 mortgage on the property which the contributing member is obligated to pay. At this point, his tax basis in his $100,000 ownership interest in the partnership is $65,000 ($20,000 cash plus $45,000 basis in property). Let us continue.

Once title to the $80,000 property item is taken over by the partnership, the property belongs to all members of the LLC. In our case, suppose that three other members assumed $30,000 of the contributing member's $40,000 mortgage debt. His tax basis in the property is now reduced to $15,000 ($45,000 initially minus $30,000 of his mortgage debt assumed by others). At this point, he has an *adjusted* tax basis of $35,000 ($20,000 money plus $15,000 basis in property) in a partnership interest worth $100,000. Doesn't sound right, does it?

But it is right. Had the contributing member subsequently liquidated his $100,000 partnership interest for $100,000 cash, he would pay tax on $65,000 ($100,000 liquidating value minus $35,000 adjusted tax basis).

As partnership operational time and activities go on, a member's adjusted tax basis in his partnership interest can, and often does, change. If he contributes additional money, or contributes property which has a basis different from its market value, his tax basis in his partnership interest will increase. Conversely, if he takes money or property out of the partnership, his tax basis will decrease. If there is an allocation to him of income or gain from the partnership operation, he pays tax on that allocation. If, upon paying the tax, he lets the allocated amounts "roll over" in the partnership (without withdrawing them), his adjusted tax basis will increase.

Somewhere down the road, a member recovers his adjusted tax base. When he does so, it is called: *return of capital*. Said return is tax FREE!

Whose responsibility is it to keep track of the various adjustments to a member's tax basis in his LLC partnership interest? It is **not** the responsibility of the partnership. The partnership has its own basis accounting problems. The responsibility rests solely and exclusively with each LLC member. If, as an LLC member, you do not keep comprehensive basis records on your own, the IRS will assert that your tax basis is zero. From such time on, you are ineligible for return of any capital, tax free. The partnership has to report all distributions made to you, to the IRS. Such reporting is done via Schedule K-1 prepared separately for each member (as covered in Chapter 12).

Partnership Basis Accounting

When one or more items of property are contributed by one or more LLC members to a partnership, the property or properties take on a new basis. The partnership, as an entity, now owns the property. It accepts the contributed property at its fair market value as though it had acquired the property by purchase. From then on, there may be additions to the property, subtractions from it, adjustments to it, or debt encumbrances placed on it.

The net result is that there develops an "inside basis" to property accounting — item by item. This basis accounting is separate and distinct from any outside basis that a member may have. When a partnership property item is sold to a nonpartner person or entity, income gain or loss is accounting recognized by the partnership. The partnership income and gain are passed through allocably to each partner where it is income taxed.

As you should sense by now, inside basis and outside basis accounting can become complex indeed. Much depends on the relative value of money and property contributed to the partnership; the diversity and use of property items; the number of contributing members; the relative capital interests of the members in the partnership; and the distributions of property to the members without its being sold by the partnership. The best we can do in general terms is the depiction we present in Figure 10.5. We just want you to visualize the separate basis accounting roles of the LLC members and their LLC entity in partnership form.

As justification for our Figure 10.5, we suggest that you glance back at Figure 10.1 (on page 10-4) for a moment. Of the 29 listings there, 10 have the word "basis" in their titles. The 10 are—

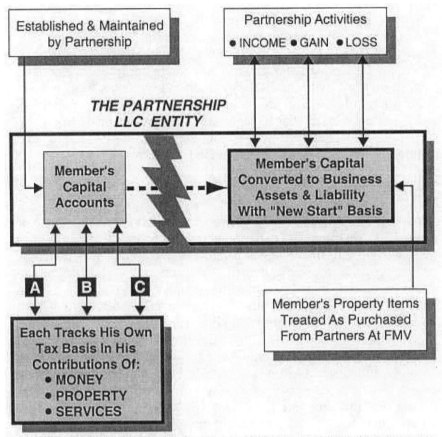

Fig. 10.5 - Separate Accounting Between LLC Members & Their Partnership

Sec. 754 — Manner of Electing Optional Adjustment to *Basis* of Partnership Property

Sec. 755 — Rules for Allocation of *Basis*

Related to, but omitted from the above 10 basis sections, are Section 721: *Nonrecognition of Gain or Loss on Contribution*; Section 731: *Extent of Recognition of Gain or Loss on Distribution*; and Section 741: *Recognition and Character of Gain or Loss on Sale or Exchange* (of one member's interest to another member in the LLC partnership). These three gain or loss sections highlight the significance of basis accounting and tracking for property disposition to, from, within, and outside the partnership arrangement. Accordingly, we touch on each one of these three sections separately below.

Contributions TO Partnership LLC

Section 721: *Nonrecognition of Gain or Loss on Contribution*, states the obvious. No gain or loss is tax recognized either to the partnership LLC or to any of its members upon the contribution of property, including money, to the partnership. This nonrecognition aspect derives from characterizing the contributory transaction as an equal-value **exchange**. That is, a member exchanges money and property for an *ownership interest* in the partnership. The value of his ownership interest in dollars is exactly the same as that of the money and property (at fair market value) contributed. The rule applies whether a new partnership is being formed or an existing partnership is seeking new capital.

Let us illustrate this nonrecognition/nontaxable concept in the simplest of terms. A member-to-be contributes property worth $10,000 to a partnership in exchange for a $10,000 ownership interest therein. His basis in that property is $4,000. Had he sold the property to a nonpartner, he would have had to pay tax on a $6,000 gain ($10,000 value – $4,000 basis). Instead, the tax is deferred until his partnership interest itself is disposed of . . . whenever. Thus, the partnership has received "built-in gain" property. But this has tax meaning only to the LLC member.

Conversely, property is contributed which has a market value of $4,000 and a tax basis of $10,000. There is a "built-in loss" here of $6,000 ($4,000 value – $10,000 basis). This, too, is not tax recognized until the member's ownership interest in the partnership is liquidated and his tax basis redetermined.

The Section 721 nonrecognition-on-contribution rule is modified in two situations. As an example of the first situation, suppose that in the $10,000 built-in gain property above, instead of a $10,000 ownership interest, the contributor received an $8,000 ownership interest. An amount of $2,000 in cash was returned to him. He pays tax on $1,200 of said amount [$2,000 proceeds minus (2/10 x $4,000 basis)]. His adjusted basis in the $8,000 partnership interest is now $3,200 [$4,000 minus (2/10 x $4,000 recognized basis)].

The second situation modifying Section 721 is where personal services are contributed in lieu of money or property. For example, an existing member's ownership interest is $8,000 (with a basis of $5,000). He has performed personal services to the partnership equivalent to $2,000 gross pay. Instead of receiving a paycheck for this amount, he wants to exchange it for a $2,000 additional capital interest. He can do this, of course, but **not** tax free. He has to pay income tax and social security/medicare tax on the entire $2,000. When he does so, his tax basis in his now $10,000 ownership interest is increased by $2,000 (from $5,000 basis to $7,000).

Distributions FROM Partnership LLC

Section 731: *Extent of Recognition of Gain or Loss on Distribution*, addresses the gain or loss recognition on distributions of partnership property. The law itself is comprised of about 1,200 statutory words. It is accompanied by some 4,000 regulatory words plus over 13,000 words of explanatory text by leading tax authorities. It is truly a formidable accounting and analysis task to distinguish between those distributions which are taxable and those which are not taxable. All that we can do here, therefore, is to synopsize the general principles underlying Section 731.

First off, there are two types of distributions from a partnership to its partners. There are *current* distributions and *liquidating* distributions. A current distribution is that which is made from the earnings and profits generated by the partnership. These distributions are taxable, or at least, tax accountable. A liquidating distribution is a redemption of part or all of a member's ownership interest in the partnership. Whether made periodically or in a lump sum, all distributions are treated as having been made at the end of the partnership's taxable accounting year.

In the most generalized sense possible, distributions of ownership capital (money and property) are not taxable except to the extent that the amount of money or marketable securities exceeds the member's adjusted basis in the partnership capital.

Section 731(a)(1) makes it clear that when any money is distributed that exceeds a member's adjusted basis in the partnership (immediately before the distribution) it is taxable. The problem is, the term "money" means more than a check made payable from the partnership's bank account. The term includes marketable securities (actively traded financial instruments). The term also includes *constructive cash distributions*. Constructive cash occurs when a member's share of partnership liabilities is reduced; when the partnership cancels a loan owed to it by a member; when the partnership expends funds on a member's behalf; and when a nonpartner owing money to the partnership instead pays it directly to a member. All of these constructive cash distributions are taxable as ordinary income to the distributee member. The partnership, therefore, must take heed and report correctly to the IRS all such monetary distributions.

Distributions of property are another matter. Where a distribution consists solely of property *other than* money, constructive cash, or marketable securities, it generally will not produce taxable gain or loss for the member. Instead, the gain or loss inherent in the property is deferred until the member actually sells or exchanges it with a nonpartner. The distributee member is on the "honor system" to preserve his tax basis in said property.

Transfer of Partnership Interest

A partnership interest is a *unit of property* in and of its own. It is some determinable fraction or percentage of the total capitalization of the business. Suppose, for example, that an LLC member's interest is 30% of the partnership's capital. He can sell all or a portion of this to an existing member. Or, he can sell to an outsider who becomes a member by purchase of all or part of the 30% interest. This is not an exchange in the sense of a distributional liquidation between partnership and member. It is a transaction solely between one LLC member and another LLC member. It's fully tax recognized to the selling member. This is the essence of Section 741: *Recognition and Character of Gain or Loss on Sale or Exchange* of partnership interest.

Section 741 goes on to say—

Such gain or loss shall be . . . from the sale or exchange of a capital asset, except as otherwise provided in section 751 (relating to unrealized receivables and inventory items).

In other words, when selling a partnership interest to another LLC member, the "unit of property" being transferred has *two* tax characteristics. One is that of a capital asset: called Section 1221 property (*Capital Asset Defined*). The second characteristic is ordinary income property: called Section 751 (*Unrealized Receivables and Inventory Items*). The term "unrealized receivables" means goods delivered or to be delivered, or services rendered or to be rendered, to the extent not previously included in income. The term "inventory items" means items on hand at the close of the taxable year held primarily for sale to customers.

Thus, the transferring member's tax basis in his partnership interest has to be apportioned between Section 1221 property and Section 751 property comparable to that which exists in the partnership itself. Section 1221 property gets capital gain/loss treatment, whereas Section 751 property gets ordinary income/loss treatment.

11

LLC OPERATING AGREEMENT

> **The Most Missed Opportunity Of An LLC Is The Failure To Formulate An Effective Operating Agreement With Vested Power In The Members. This Means Setting Such Conditions As: (1) Initial Capitalization, (2) Books Of Account, (3) Managing Member, (4) Rules Committee (For New Members), (5) Capital Account Balances, (6) Guaranteed Payments, (7) Ordinary Losses, (8) Passive Activity Losses, (9) Capital Losses, And (10) Supplemental Agreements. When Consensus-Adopted, The Master Agreement Sets The Stage For Distributive Sharing Among Members Of All Items Of Income, Deductions, Credits, Etc. . . . Each Year.**

A Multi-Member LLC has one unique problem. Each member, whether domestic or foreign, is a "capital owner." This means that each member has managerial rights and management say on his/her/its own. This is analogous to each member having his own proprietorship form of business. When there are just two or three — or even four — co-equal managers, the LLC arrangement can function quite well. An oral agreement and a few handshakes are all that are needed.

But when the 5th member comes on board . . . or the 100th, the acceptance of management co-equality breaks down. What then?

Answer: This is where an operating agreement in WRITING — becomes a MUST. Even among the best of close friends, disharmony and disruption of the business take place when there are too many equal-say managers. At some point, a written operating agreement must be formulated. To be legally binding, the agreement must be read, understood, and signed by all members joining the LLC enterprise at the time of its adoption.

It is the innate (inherent) power within a group of associating individuals to agree among themselves how "things" — their money, property, services, and say — shall be managed in an orderly fashion. This is not a concession of state law nor of federal law. It is the right of *informed consent* to which all human beings are privileged.

What are the contents of an LLC Operating Agreement?

This is where both state law and federal law are silent. Because of this silence, each LLC has to wing it on its own. Consequently, what follows in this chapter is an effort to set forth certain practical operating rules that, we believe, are conducive to good managerial, fiscal, and tax control of a successful LLC. The points presented can be adopted, altered, amended, or rescinded as each LLC experience unfolds.

Meaning of Statutory Silence

It is instructive to review briefly what state and federal laws say on the subject of operating agreements for LLCs and for partnerships.

For our state law example, we again rely on the California Corporation Code. Its Section 17059 reads verbatim as—

> *Operating agreement: The power to adopt, alter, amend, or repeal the operating agreement of a limited liability company shall be vested in the members. The articles of organization or a written operating agreement may prescribe the manner in which the operating agreement may be altered, amended, or repealed.*

That's it! No requirements whatsoever are prescribed for the contents of such an agreement.

The crucial clause to note is: *The power to . . . is vested in* (the members). If this power is ignored or misused, the LLC members have only themselves to blame for entity wrongdoings. These include wanton mismanagement, intrusion of con artistry, harassing lawsuits, and punitive tax penalties. The members also have it within their power to manage the entity prudently and to discipline those members who abuse their participative rights.

The Internal Revenue Code (federal law) pretty well echoes the context silence above. IRC Section 761(c): *Partnership Agreement*, says in key part that—

> *For purposes of* [Subchapter K] *a partnership agreement includes any modifications . . . made prior to, or at, the time prescribed for filing the partnership return for the taxable year.* [The "prescribed date" is April 15th, generally.]

Subchapter K (Partners and Partnerships) was that which we covered in Chapter 10. Regulation § 1.701-2(a): *Anti-abuse rule*, refers to the implication of Subchapter K where the partnership operations . . .

> *must accurately reflect the partners' economic agreement.*

Regulation §1.761-1(c): *Terms defined*, points out that—

> *As to any matter which the partnership agreement . . . is silent, the provisions of local law shall be considered to constitute a part of the agreement.*

Here, the term "local law" pertains to city, county, and state laws that are applicable to all businesses operating within their jurisdictions.

Where does this statutory silence on the contents of an operating agreement leave us?

Answer: Every LLC is on its own. A reasonable goal would be to create a fallback document that all signatory members could rely on when controversies arise. We can visualize four particular areas of controversy, namely:

1. Fending off con artists,
2. Treatment of customers and suppliers,
3. Oversight of members' capital accounts, and
4. Ushering out dissenters and malcontents.

In Figure 11.1, we present a philosophical depiction of how these controversies might relate to an LLC operating agreement.

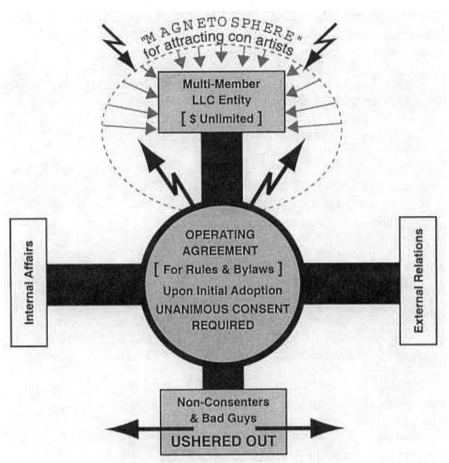

Fig. 11.1 - The Philosophical Role of an LLC Operating Agreement

Introductory Considerations

The operating agreement, first and foremost, should comprise practical guidelines for conducting the internal affairs of business. It should be concise and comprehensible, spanning no more than two or three pages. It should not be in "small print" nor be in legalese. It is intended to be read before signing.

Before any signatures are affixed, a draft should be prepared and passed around for comment. The draft should be prepared by one or more members with an aptitude for business writing and some familiarity with contract formulation. After the draft is semi-finalized, have it reviewed by an attorney familiar with LLC law in your home state. Do not let the attorney completely rewrite the draft, as it will be blown into a formal legal — obfuscating — document. Such a document would intimidate members and turn them away. Yet, you need one or two attorneys on tap for that inevitable day when some nasty lawsuit will erupt out of the blue.

Basically, what the agreement should portray is a common sense roadmap for conducting business in an above-board manner. You can't run a business objectively if you are constantly worrying about a lawsuit. If you do, you soon become paranoid, which translates into irrational distrust of others. There'll be paranoia enough when contending with the IRS, its Subchapter K rules, and with corresponding state agencies. Don't overblow regulatory concerns. Go about your business of treating members, customers, suppliers, and employees with fairness and friendliness.

The model of simplicity and common sense that we envision in an operating agreement is presented in Figure 11.2. The presentation is just a model; it is not a final document by any stretch. For space reasons, we show only three members. As rationalized above, start the written process at five members and provide means for expanding the list up to some anticipated maximum number (less than 100). If there are too many capital-contributors, the whole management process breaks down with internal bickering on money matters.

Entry Rules for Newcomers

Note that the last item in Figure 11.2 is the consensus designation of a Managing Member (or General Manager). Such a person should have at least a 20% capital ownership in the LLC entity. His objective, and that of all the founding/forming members, should be to attract as many capital contributing members as are necessary and prudent for the core business intended. This means establishing a Rules Committee to set the ground rules for new members coming on board.

LLC OPERATING AGREEMENT

This AGREEMENT is made between
_____ , (called Member "A")
_____ , (called Member "B")
and _____ , (called Member "C")

These parties voluntarily associate themselves together as LLC
Members for the purpose of conducting the business of _____
_____
_____ .

Name & Duration: The name of the LLC shall be _____
_____ . The entity shall continue
until dissolved by mutual consent or as otherwise terminated.

Place of Business: The principal place of business shall be
_____ and such other place or places
as may be mutually agreed upon.

Initial Capital: The initial capital of the LLC entity shall be
$_____ , and each member shall contribute as follows:

    Member "A" $_____ *(or the equivalent)*
    Member "B" $_____ *(or the equivalent)*
    Member "C" $_____ *(or the equivalent)*

Books of Account: The LLC shall keep accurate, up-to-
date, and complete books of account at all times. Said books shall be
open to examination by any member.

Managing Member: The members mutually agree that _____
_____ (Member "A") shall act as General Manager to
oversee all business affairs including the preparation of books of account,
all tax returns, and all other documents pertaining to the business.

WITNESSED BY	Executed at _____ on _____
Notary (seal) *Public* _____	_____ , Member "A" _____ , Member "B" _____ , Member "C"

Fig. 11.2 - Introductory Points in a Simplified LLC Agreement

The Rules Committee should be comprised of no less than three members, and no more than five or seven, depending on membership size. It would be charged with screening new members and interrogating them with respect to their capital participation capabilities. The idea is to seek material participants who have the know-how and business talent or contacts to help the business grow. The idea also is to screen out purely passive investors, con artists, and scam operators. Interrogation includes carefully (and diplomatically) questioning each new member's origin of money, property, or services that he or she intends to offer to the LLC in exchange for an ownership interest therein.

As to contributing money, the policy should be: No "green paper" cash or gold coins accepted. Cash provides no trail to its origin. The acceptance of cash risks being drawn into money laundering schemes that can lead to endless probing by regulatory, legal, and taxing agencies. Instead of cash, insist on a cashier's check, personal check, or money order. These instruments provide an origin trail, should it be needed.

As to contributing property, the policy of acceptance should be based on its *equity value*. The term "equity value" means the property's fair market value (FMV) **minus** all debt encumbrances (mortgages, deeds of trust, promissory notes, judicial assessments, tax liens, etc.). The idea is not to become bogged down with "problem property" that is not useful in the LLC business itself, nor readily convertible to other more useful property, nor convertible to monetary forms. Any offering of problem property is a tip-off to the behavioral character of the offerer.

With the above generalities in mind, the next item in an LLC operating agreement could include—

Rules Committee. Each new member's contributory offering in money, property, or services, shall be examined, verified, and quantified in dollar value. Upon acceptance of the dollar amount by the Rules Committee, the offerer shall be issued a Certificate of Ownership Interest, properly dated.

Maintaining Capital Accounts

The greatest weakness of an LLC enterprise is its starvation of capital. This starvation comes about because of the widespread belief that the LL (limited liability) shield protects all members against any failure of the entity to meet its operating obligations. This is a fallacy in protection thinking which we've tried to expose in preceding chapters.

The general accounting rule for fiscal responsibility in any business is quite straightforward. We portrayed it, we believe, in Figure 10.3 on page 10-11 and in the surrounding text (on pages 10-8 through page 10-13, particularly). The rule is that, at the end of each accounting period, the capital on hand (money in the bank) plus the quick-sale value (within 90 days) of marketable assets must cover all operating liabilities of the enterprise. Any shortfalls in this regard are a cause of management concern.

A prudent operating policy for any bona fide LLC is the mandatory restoration of each member's capital account, when it becomes delinquent. An account is delinquent when its balance at the end of each accounting period is zero or negative.

What happens if a member has a shortfall in his/her/its capital account balance?

Answer: There are four courses of action, namely:

1. Direct (in writing) that the delinquent account be restored to a positive amount within 90 days.

2. If effort 1 fails, notify the delinquent account holder that he is no longer recognized as a valid member of the LLC. Provide him one more opportunity to restore his balance before the end of the tax accounting year.

3. If effort 2 fails, engage an attorney to prepare an Account Past Due demand and address it to the delinquent member.

4. If effort 3 fails, have a law firm prepare and serve a Breach of Contract lawsuit against the delinquent member.

With the above in mind, the next item in a Figure 11.2-type operating agreement could include—

Capital Accounts. At the end of each calendar quarter (namely March 31, June 30, September 30, and December 31), the capital account of each member shall be posted and certified. Where a member has a zero or negative balance, he shall be given 90 days to restore his balance to a positive amount. If he does not do so, he shall be subject to disciplinary action and, possibly also, to legal action.

Self-Employment Earnings

There is one item that is guaranteed to generate controversy in an LLC operation. Said item pertains to what constitutes self-employment earnings in the day-to-day activities of the LLC's core business. No active trade or business will function by itself alone. Some body or bodies must run the store. Since all members are capital owners of the business, one or more such members must participate on a day-to-day basis to keep the business alive and successful. Those who do so are compensated by what are called: *self-employment earnings.*

But there's a catch. Self-employment earnings are subject to a self-employment (SE) tax. Without other personal service income, the SE tax is a flat 15.3% combined rate for social security and medicare taxation purposes. The SE tax does not sit well with those who have fanciful delusions of "limited liability" in a free-wheeling entrepreneurial world.

For example, suppose that Member X is a 10% capital owner of the business and that he devotes 500 hours or more for the year to its daily activities. His distributive share of the earnings and profits amounts to $80,000. How much are self-employment earnings and how much constitutes profit on his capital investment?

There is no fixed answer. The IRS has yet to propose some rational guideline on this issue for LLCs. The IRS would prefer that the maximum possible be attributable to self-employment earnings. There would be more tax this way.

One approach would be to value a member's personal services proportional to the like-kind compensation paid to employees in non-LLC businesses. Hours proportionality would also be used. An ordinary work year is 2,000 hours (50 wks x 40 hrs/wk). Thus, if an LLC member worked 500 hours and his non-LLC counterpart earned $60,000 a year, the LLC member could be assigned $15,000 (1/4 of $60,000) as "comparable earnings."

Even so, the SE earnings amount would have to be negotiated between the member and his entity. The member would want the amount to be as low as possible (to minimize the 15.3% SE tax).

The entity would want the hours of service to be as high as possible, to protect its financial interests. An owner-member who works in the LLC business is more likely to safeguard the entity's interests than would a non-owner employee.

In the end, some form of *guaranteed payment* would have to be negotiated. This would mean including in the Figure 11.2 operating agreement such wording as—

> Guaranteed Payments. All members are expected to contribute their personal services to the success of the LLC entity. Those who devote more than 500 hours per year of their personal time are deserving of special consideration. For such individuals, a "guaranteed payment" shall be prescribed. Such payments shall constitute self-employment earnings that are subject to the self-employment tax: Schedule SE (Form 1040). Such payments are a priority expenditure of the business before its net earnings and profits are established.

There is a special reason why we prescribe guaranteed payments in the operating agreement. The LLC and its members beat the IRS to the draw. Nothing defeats IRS aggressiveness more than being prepared for its negative rulings ahead of time.

Self-Employment Losses

With regard to self-employment income, the IRS has devised seven "material participation" tests for determining such income. Test 1 — the guiding star — is 500 or more hours of personal services for the year. Test 2 — the distant star — is 100 or more hours but less than 500 hours of personal service. The other five tests are IRS judgment calls based on other facts and circumstances. This is all fine when the core business of an LLC generates positive income at its bottom line.

What happens if, instead of positive income, there is negative income — called: *ordinary loss* — at the bottom line? This is where internal controversies **will arise** concerning those guaranteed payments to some members. Said payments may indeed cause a loss, whereas without them there might be no loss. Let us explain.

Page 1 of Form 1065: *U.S. Return of LLC Income* is an ordinary profit or loss statement for an unincorporated business. It consists of seven income entry lines and 12 expense deduction lines. the first deduction line is: *Salaries and wages (other than to members).* The second deduction line is: *Guaranteed payments to members.* The other 10 deduction lines are those expenses allowable to any business, whether an LLC or not. Our Figure 11.3 may be helpful to you at this point. Note that the bottom line therein is designated: ***Ordinary income <loss>.***

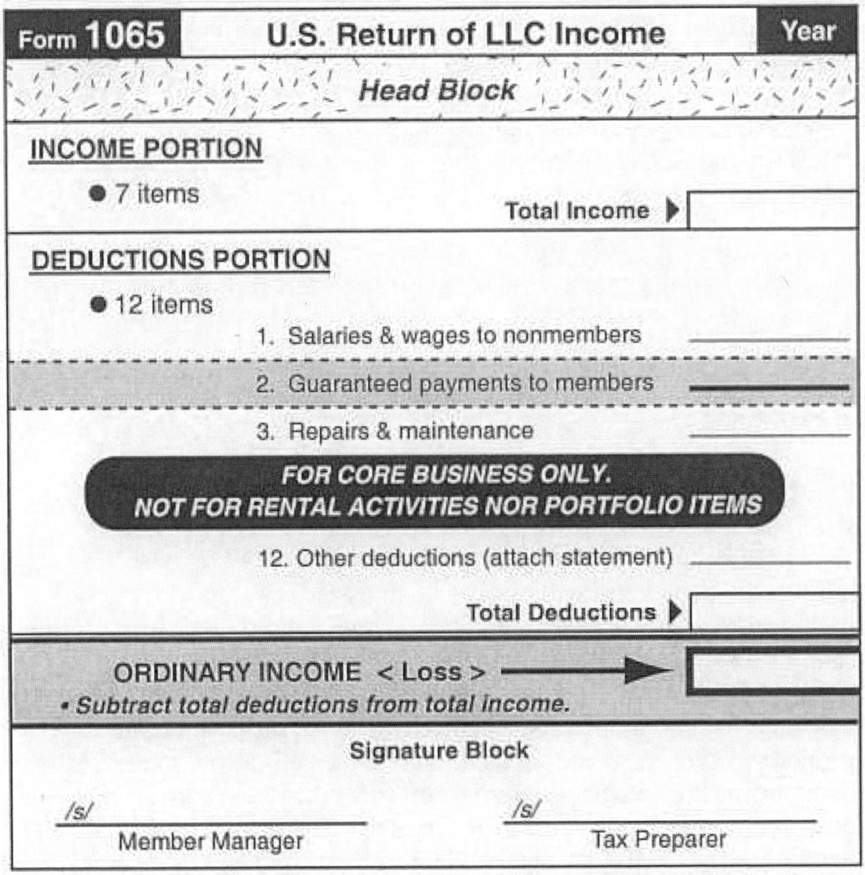

Form **1065**	**U.S. Return of LLC Income**	Year

Head Block

INCOME PORTION

● 7 items

Total Income ▶

DEDUCTIONS PORTION

● 12 items

1. Salaries & wages to nonmembers _____

2. Guaranteed payments to members _____

3. Repairs & maintenance _____

**FOR CORE BUSINESS ONLY.
NOT FOR RENTAL ACTIVITIES NOR PORTFOLIO ITEMS**

12. Other deductions (attach statement) _____

Total Deductions ▶

ORDINARY INCOME < Loss > ⟶

• Subtract total deductions from total income.

Signature Block

/s/ _____   /s/ _____
Member Manager   Tax Preparer

Fig. 11.3 - The Deduction Role of "Guaranteed Payments" to LLC Members

Obviously, if the guaranteed payments are too high, relatively, they could drive a marginal business into negative/loss territory. This would not sit well with other owner-members who have their own capital on the line.

One solution is to offer those members who devote 100 or more hours (but less than 500 hours) to the business an allocable portion of the loss as: *self-employment loss.* Those working less than 100 hours or more than 500 hours would not participate in such loss.

Why do we suggest this offering? Simple answer. A self-employment loss, when passed through to each allocable member, can be used to offset all other sources of a member's income on Form 1040: ***U.S. Individual Income Tax Return.*** Unlike other types of losses that pass through, a self-employment loss is not subject to loss limitation rules.

With the above in mind, the next inclusion in a Figure 11.2-type operating agreement could be—

> Ordinary Losses. When the entity's core business (on page 1 of Form 1065) results in a loss instead of a profit, such loss shall be deemed a "self-employment loss." The members participating in this loss shall be those who have devoted 100 hours or more, but less than 500 hours, of their personal services to the business. The allocation percentages used for SE loss purposes shall have no effect on other types of pass-throughs of the enterprise.

Passive Activity Losses

In addition to its core (self-employment type) business, an LLC may engage in passive activity businesses. A "passive activity" includes rental real estate and other rental activities where renting/leasing the underlying asset (building, land, equipment) is the principal source of income. Personal services therewith are confined to management oversight and property maintenance. The property used in these activities is allowed attractive statutory deductions known as depreciation (of buildings, structures, and equipment) and as *depletion* (of natural deposits in, on, and deep below land). Depreciation and depletion allowances by themselves often can produce passive activity losses.

A passive activity carries with it an adverse implication. The premise is that, in such an activity, the property owners are motivated more by its tax benefits (depreciation, etc.) than by ordinary income seeking. To address this implication, there is IRC Section 469: ***Passive Activity Losses . . . Limited.*** Its 5,000-word thesis is a flat-out disallowance of all losses — unless certain conditions are met.

There are three such conditions. One, the manager/overseer must be actively engaged in all inquiries and decisions regarding the use and care of the property. He or she must be available when needed, irrespective of the hours involved. Two, the manager/overseer must be at least a 10% owner of the property (or properties) being rented. This requirement holds that the true owner of property will be more protective of it than a nonowner manager. And, three, the manager/owner is permitted to claim up to $25,000 in passive losses of his/her Form 1040 AGI (adjusted gross income) if less than $100,000 [IRC Sec. 469(i)]. The $25,000 allowable loss is phased out at the rate of 50 cents for every dollar of AGI over $100,000. Thus, at or over $150,000 AGI, no passive losses are allowed.

The "up to" $25,000 passive loss allowance creates a pass-through challenge for LLC members. If there were 10 members, each holding a 10% ownership interest in the LLC entity, could the entity pass through up to $250,000 in passive losses? That would be $25,000 separately for each of 10 members.

You should know instinctively that the IRS would not allow such an arrangement. Actually, there is no clear statutory prohibition against the 10 times $25,000 loss pass-through for LLCs. Nevertheless, the IRS would insist that all LLC members are "closely related" (businesswise) and, therefore, are treatable as *one taxpayer* (for Section 469(a) purposes). We get some support for this thinking from Regulation § 1.469-5T(e): *Treatment of limited partners.* A less than 10% LLC member is treated as a limited partner who is allowed no passive loss pass-throughs whatsoever. Thus, our conclusion is that an LLC with passive rental activities would be limited to one $25,000 pass-through loss each year. Any net rental loss greater than $25,000 would be carried over within the LLC to the following year.

With the above commentary in mind, the next inclusion in a Figure 11.2-type operating agreement could be—

Passsive Activity Losses. Should the entity incur any rental real estate and/or other rental activity losses, said losses aggregating no more than $25,000 shall be passed through, prorata, to each 10% or more owner-member actively participating in said activities.

Portfolio Capital Losses

A "portfolio" is dictionary-defined as: *A group of investments held by an investor or financial institution.* An "investor," in turn, is defined as: *One who commits money in order to gain profit . . . or interest . . . or dividends.* Thus, a portfolio consists of an assortment of paper (intangible) assets such as stock, bonds, debt instruments, and fractional ownership interests in other pass-through entities. Only money (capital) is at stake. No personal services are performed; no rental activities are involved.

When a portfolio asset is sold or exchanged, the result is capital gain, capital loss, or return of capital (neither gain nor loss). All investors know this. Obviously, capital gains are preferred. When passed through to LLC members, said gains — generally, without limit — are allowed preferential tax treatment; namely, a 15% rate versus a 35% rate (ordinarily). There is, however, a 25% rate for unrecaptured gain and a 28% rate for collectibles gain.

What happens when there are capital losses to be passed through? Is there any pass-through limitation on the amount of these losses? What if there were $250,000 in capital losses?

Answer: No; there is no capital loss limitation at the entity level. There is a natural reason for this. For their own self-interest, investors invest for profit. They do not invest for loss, as they might with rental activities with large depreciation allowances and other deductions against income.

At the individual distributee level, there is a capital loss limitation rule. Said rule is Section 1211: *Limitation on Capital Losses.* The limitation amount is $3,000 in net losses, after offsets for capital gains for the taxable year. Any excess capital losses beyond $3,000 may be carried over and combined with subsequent year capital gains and losses. Except for death, etc., there is no limitation in the number of carryover years.

With the foregoing in mind, the next inclusion in an LLC operating agreement could be—

Capital Losses. Regardless of the amount, all portfolio-type capital losses shall be passed through to each member in proportion to his/her/its capital balances at the end of the entity's tax accounting year. Each member thereafter is on his own with respect to the $3,000 per year loss limitation rule of Section 1211, U.S. Tax Code.

Newsletter Transparency

Congress and the IRS have become increasingly sensitive to potential tax abuses by pass-through entities: partnerships, LLCs, S corporations, and foreign trusts. Often, these entities are closely held and controlled by five or fewer principals owning more than 50% of the capital at-risk therein. Their policies and intentions tend to be secretive. Their focus is on those tax benefits and tax deductions that accrue mostly to themselves. Other capital contributors provide the backdrop for posturing as a bona fide profit-seeking enterprise.

The IRS has postulated various "tests" that seek to distinguish between a tax shelter and a bona fide business. Five prevailing tests are:

Test 1 — A significant portion of the arrangement is the avoidance or evasion of tax via exclusions from gross income, nonrecognition of gain, tax credits, adjustments (or the absence thereof) to basis of property, contrived losses, etc.

Test 2 — The tax shelter ratio (of benefits to capital) is greater than 2 to 1 for each of the first five years of operation.

Test 3 — An investment of more than $250,000 is on the line from at least five contributors, often for brief periods of 45 days or less at a time.

Test 4 — The ownership interests are in a form and amount which are exempt from registration under Federal and State securities laws.

Test 5 — The arrangement is offered to a certain few under conditions of confidentiality, with contractual protection if the expected tax benefits do not materialize.

In 2004, new laws (Sec. 6111), new penalties (Sec. 6707A), and new regulations (Reg. § 1.6011-4(d) were enacted to thwart the continuing emergence of tax avoidance schemes. For such schemes, the tax penalties can range from $10,000 to $100,000 for individual participants and from $50,000 to $200,000 for entity participants.

For a bona fide LLC, there's a simple way to go. That is, adopt a policy of transparency in the investment mix of activities engaged in. For example, the mix of LLC activities could be grouped into three specific categories, as we depict in Figure 11.4.

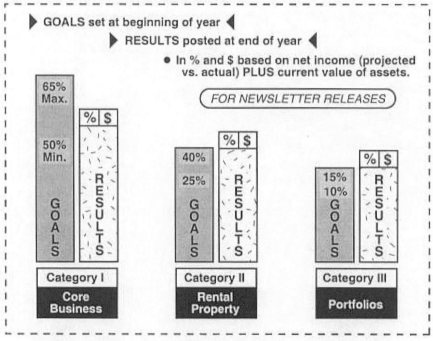

Fig. 11.4 - Newsletter Disclosure of Annual Goals & Results

Note the indication of operational goals, current year results, and the wrapping together into a year-end newsletter. A newsletter — for all to read, compare, and discuss — could be a valuable adjunct to Schedule K-1 (in the next chapter) issued to every LLC member. The idea is to sidestep confidential and secretive arrangements, and correct any expectations of unrealistic tax benefits and profit results. Published data is most helpful when confronting allegations of "oral promises."

Amendments & Alterations

An LLC Operating Agreement is a *flexible* economic instrument. It has to be so because each member is a co-owner of the business. Each co-owner is entitled to his/her/its distributive share of the tax benefits and burdens and of the financial income and deductions of the enterprise. As a flexible instrument, it can be amended, altered, and supplemented at any time. Doing so requires the consensus approval of the ongoing members. One concept in this regard is depicted in Figure 11.5.

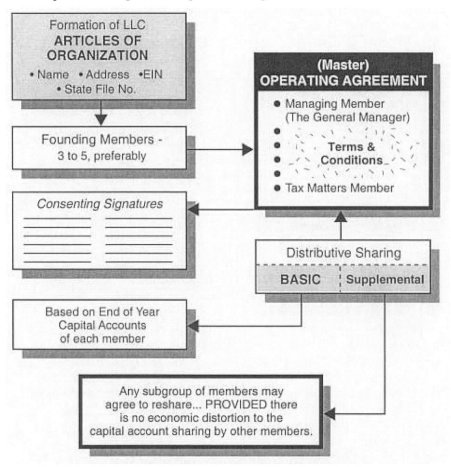

Fig. 11.5 - Distinction Between Master and Supplemental Agreements

There should be only one LLC person responsible for coordinating, posting, and clarifying all changes to the operating agreement. The logical person for this task is the *Tax Matters Member* (TMM). This is an owner-member with some accounting background who oversees the preparation of all tax returns and of all financial statements for the enterprise. His or her name is a required designation on page 2 (bottom) of Form 1065: *U.S. Return of LLC Income*.

Among the duties expected of the TMM is the acceptance — and attachment of — supplemental agreements between any three or more members. By a "supplemental agreement" we mean that situation where less than 100% of the membership agree to switch and trade their distributive sharing items among themselves. The only condition is that they do so in a manner that causes no economic distortion to items (of income, deductions, credits, etc.) that pass through to nonparticipating supplementors. Thereafter, a supplemental agreement could be attached to the consensus-approved operating agreement as an addendum to it. Note in Figure 11.5 that the general rule for distributive sharing (touched on in Chapter 10) is proportionalized directly to the capital account balances of each member at the end of the tax accounting year. This is the basic premise for all sharing, unless altered by any subgroup of members within themselves.

It is our position that if no, or an ineffective, operating agreement is prepared, the LLC members have only themselves to blame when tax, regulatory, and/or judicial agencies set the operating conditions. Whenever any government agency gets in the act, it is a virtual guarantee that no member will be fully satisfied. Every home state LLC law recognizes the inherent power of an LLC to set the terms and conditions for its own "internal affairs." Externally, the LLC must perform like any other bona fide profit-seeking enterprise.

12

POSTING SCHEDULES K-1

No LLC Operation Is Complete Until Every Member Has Received A Schedule K-1 For The Year. A K-1 Includes Pass-Through Tax Information Such As Ordinary Income Or Loss, Rental Income Or Loss, Portfolio Income Or Loss, Allocable Credits & Deductions, Foreign Transactions, AMT (Alternative Minimum Tax) Items, Self-Employment Earnings, Etc. The Entry Amounts Are Based On Each Member's Profit, Loss, & Capital Percentages At Year End. Included Also On The K-1 Is An Analysis Of Each Member's CAPITAL ACCOUNT As It Dovetails Into The Overall Solvency Of The LLC Relative To Its Assets And Liabilities.

The head portion of Form 1065: *U.S. Return of Partnership* [LLC] *Income* has an instruction that reads—

> *Number of Schedules K-1. Attach one for each person who was* [an LLC member] *at any time during the tax year.*
> ▶ _____.

A Schedule K-1, as you probably know by now is titled: *Partner's* [LLC Member's] *Share of Income, Deductions, Credits, etc.*

Elsewhere, regulations direct that the first recipient of a K-1 shall be that person holding the largest profits-interest in the reporting entity [Reg. § 301.6231(a)(7)-1(m)(2)]. Such a person may also be designated as the *Tax Matters Member* (TMM). The presumption is that he who holds the largest financial stake in a closely-held enterprise will do most to assure that the distributive sharing items on each Schedule K-1 are "true, correct, and complete." This requires independent accounting.

Another regulation [Reg. § 301.6231(a)(7)-2(b)(3)] focuses on LLCs where only a member-manager can be treated as a general partner. Such a person is also considered to be the General Manager Member (GMM) . . .

> *who, alone or together with others, is vested with the continuing exclusive authority to make the management decisions necessary to conduct the* [profit seeking] *business for which the organization was formed.*

Our take on the above is that the GMM would sign Form 1065 . . . *Under penalties of perjury.* He would also designate the TMM (Tax Matters Member) who would prepare the tax return and all of its accompanying schedules and statements. Hence, it becomes obvious that the TMM is responsible for preparing all Schedules K-1 that attach to Form 1065. The GMM would be the No. 1 recipient of a K-1, whereas the TMM would be the No. 2 recipient.

How does the TMM do this for an LLC? That's what this, our final chapter, is about. For preparing any of the K-1s, an up-to-date master operating agreement and supplemental agreements, if any, are essential. We tried to portray in Figure 11.4 (on page 11-16) the functional distinction between the master and subagreements. We assume at this point that **you** are the TMM. We also assume that you are a conscientious K-1 oveerseer.

Getting Started

You can't do Schedules K-1 out of thin air. A lot of preceding preparatory work has to be done. This includes the completion of Form 1065 with all of its required attachments . . . except the K-1s. We covered many of these foundational activities in Chapter 6: Multi-Member LLCs and in chapter 10: Partnership LLC Rules. We need to coalesce those earlier principles and move on.

Have you draft-prepared Form 1065 yet? If so, or if not, we remind you that you need information from its following pages, forms, and schedules:

Page 1 — Income or <loss> from the core business
Page 2 — Cost of goods sold & other information
Page 3 — Members' (plural) distributive share items
- Form 8825: Rental real estate income & expenses
- Sched. D (1065): Capital gains & losses
- Form 4797: Sales of business property
- Form 4562: Depreciation & amortization
- Form 3800: General business credits
Page 4 ' Analysis of net income <loss>
- Sched. L: Balance sheets per books
- Sched. M-1: Reconciliation of books with return
- Sched. M-2: Analysis of members' capital accounts

As you can sense from the outline above, a substantial amount of information is needed before transferring it onto a separate Schedule K-1 for each member. Do not be overwhelmed by this necessity. Professional help can always be obtained. Be aware, though, that the professional term "per books" means ordinary plain language accounting: dollars in, dollars out; dollars here, dollars there. You don't need professional help for checking the day-to-day bank book balances of the LLC entity. If it's negative, you know you're in trouble.

In Figure 12.1, we present a blueprint of the balancing act required for the LLC entity overall. As you can see, it's a matter of balancing all members' capital accounts collectively with the assets and liabilities on Schedule L (page 4) of Form 1065. The quickest way to do this is to verify the Ending Balance of Schedule M-2 (in Figure 12.1). If this amount is positive, fine. If this amount is negative, not fine. If negative, it tells you that one or more members are not contributing their share of capital to the enterprise. You need to identify which member is the culprit.

You can do this identification without talking to any members directly. As the TMM, you are analyzing the books and records of the business. Included in this analysis are the capital accounts (in the business) of each member individually. We try to make you aware of this inclusion in the lower portion of Figure 12.1. Note the inclusion of Schedules K-1 in the ending balance on Schedule M-2. The K-1s, in turn, play a pivotal role in balancing the assets and liabilities of the entity.

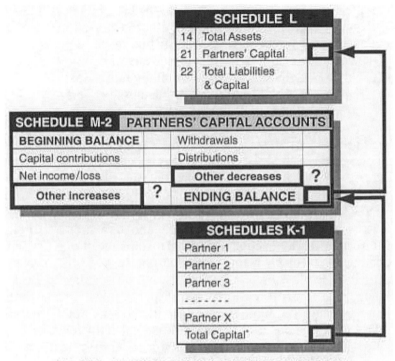

Fig. 12.1 - How the K-1s Fund an LLC's Needed Capital

Item N on Schedule K-1

On each Schedule K-1, there is an official "Item N". It is captioned: *Member's* (singular) *capital account analysis.* It is a straightforward in-and-out tracking of each member's capital increases and decreases for the year. For this tracking, your hope is that there is a separate accounting ledger for each member. And that it reflects an accurate record of that member's capital activity with annotated dates and explanations. Then, for each per member K-1, your summary would look like this:

Beginning capital account	$_____
Capital contributed during the year	_____
Current year increase <decrease>	_____
Withdrawals & distributions	_____
Ending capital account	_____

From entity records kept in dollars and with (tax) basis rules when property or services are involved, you reconstruct the capital account for each member. If there are five members, you do this five times. If there are 25 members, you do the capital reconstruction 25 times. Sooner or later, one or more members will emerge as having a negative (below zero) ending balance. If negative, it must be restored to zero or above. This is the *Economic substance rule* that we addressed on pages 10-6 through 10-12 of Chapter 10.

As the TMM, give yourself a little practice on the item N entries. Do so by reconstructing first your own capital account. You do not want to be in the embarrassing position of confronting other members with negative balances when your own capital account is negative.

Next, check out the GMM's (General Manager Member's) end-of-year capital account balance. If his is negative, you'd best have a private conversation with him. As the business grows and develops, it is the general manager who will have to "enforce" the operationally agreed-to positive balances. If his is negative and he shows no inclination to correct his own, you — as the Tax Matters Member — may want to rethink your affiliation with the LLC.

Particularly so, if the general manager says that he has read the instructions to item N and finds that doing item N is not necessary. Indeed, the item N instructions say in part—

You are not required to complete item N if . . .

   (1)   The total receipts [from all LLC activities] *were less than $250,000 **and** (2) the total assets* [for all LLC activities] *were less than $600,000 . . . at the end of each accounting year.*

Our position is that, leaving item N blank — even when permitted to do so — introduces the element of sloppiness into the accounting affairs of the enterprise. Any sloppiness in LLC accounting is a guaranteed target for probing in the event of a lawsuit. It is better to have an affirmative defense against such probing, by completing item N at all times. One never knows when a lawsuit will strike. If and when it does, negative and zero capital account members will vanish into thin air. The more responsible members will be left holding the bag.

The Checkboxes at Item N

Just below the last dollar entry in item N, there are four checkboxes. They are captioned:

☐ *Tax basis*   ☐ *Section 704(b) book*

☐ *GAAP*   ☐ *Other (explain)*

Without understanding fully what these checkboxes mean, you should sense that they have something to do with the capital accounting process for each member. And they do.

The instructions to the checkboxes imply that you could check a different box for different members (if applicable). Doing so would lead to controversy between the different members. One or more would claim to be underadvantaged relative to others. Furthermore, as Figure 12.1 implies, there has to be capital accounting uniformity among all members. Hence, we urge that, whichever box is checked for Member 1, it also be checked for Member X . . . and all those in between.

The instructions for checking the boxes are not usefully informative. The term "Tax basis" means capital accounting identical with that used for income and deductions on Form 1065 for the entity overall. The term "704(b) book" means the capital accounting rules under Regulation § 1.704-1(b)(2)(iv) involving nearly 70 pages of small print text. The "GAAP" box means generally accepted accounting principles . . . whatever they are. The "Other" box allows you to explain (via an attached statement) how each of the entry lines in the capital account was determined.

We have a two-pronged position on which boxes to check. If you simply want to appease the IRS's computer, check the "GAAP" box and hope no LLC member will ask you to explain. If you want to satisfy the LLC members that you are being uniform and fair, check the "Other" box. This will permit you to explain how any specifically allocated items are handled.

For example, capital gains and losses are reported as separate transactions on Schedule D (Form 1065). On Schedule K, they are short-term netted and, separately, also long-term netted. When passed through onto Schedule K-1, each netting may be specifically allocated to certain members as per terms of the operating agreement. Consequently, for certain members, the item N *current year increase <decrease>* will have to be explained. You might as well do all explaining in a separate attachment in anticipation of member challenges. Thus, when in doubt, check the "Other" box . . . and explain.

Items L and M on Schedule K-1

Less controversial, perhaps, are items L and M on each member's Schedule K-1. These are matters generally agreed to in the operating agreement. If not in the master agreement, then surely in a supplemental agreement. Any subgroup of members can reshare their profit and loss percentages without economic distortion to others. Item **L** is captioned—

Member's share of profit, loss, and capital:

	Beginning	*Ending*
Profit	_____ %	_____ %
Loss	_____ %	_____ %
Capital	_____ %	_____ %

The instructions to item L dwell mostly on the beginning entries when there has been a change of the profit or loss sharing during the year. Any change is treated as a new beginning for each member so affected. If there are multiple changes during the year, attach a statement describing the dates and percentages before and after each change. Otherwise, as the TMM, assure yourself that the percentages you use are covered in the operating agreement or in other attachments thereto. These percentages, within the economic substance rule, need not be related to the capital percentages of ownership interests in the entity.

On the line for *Capital* (percentages), the instructions say—

Enter the portion of capital that the member would receive if the entity were liquidated by distributing all assets and liabilities of the entity [as edited for LLCs].

This gets us back to the message in Figure 12.1 where all members own the assets and liabilities of the entity. That is, each member owns proportionately his capital account percentage of the business. Thus, as a fallback position, if the profit and loss percentages are unrealistic or are controversial, the capital account percentages prevail.

The item M is captioned—

Member's share of liabilities at year end:

Nonrecourse	$_____
Qualified nonrecourse financing	$_____
Recourse	$_____

A pure nonrecourse liability is passé these days. The term "nonrecourse" means that the LLC assumes a loan for which no member bears the economic risk of loss. What financial institution is going to lend real money to an enterprise — especially an LLC — where there's no chance of suing for recovery of that money? Because nonrecourse loans are structured to be self-canceling, they are the *paper weapon of choice* for scam artists. The "Irving scheme," starting on page 9-4, is a classic example of what can be at stake for unsuspecting members.

Qualified nonrecourse financing requires that real property (land, buildings, natural resources) be collateral for the loan. If the LLC entity owns said property, and the loan is not paid off when due, the lender takes over the property. Thereafter, no LLC member is liable. This means that all members lose their capital investment in the qualified property. Members who contributed the property initially have a basis adjustment to make.

Amounts "At Risk" Explained

Without explaining so on Schedule K-1, item M above is directed at the at-risk concerns of IRC Section 465. This 3,600-

word sectioon of the tax code is titled: ***Deductions Limited to Amount at Risk***. What kind of deductions are limited?

Short answer: Loss-type deductions. An LLC can pass through to its members various losses proportional to the loss percentages agreed to or, if no such agreement, proportional to each member's capital account. Thus, one way to increase one's loss pass-throughs is to voluntarily share disproportionately some of the indebtedness of the entity. If a loss pass-through meets the statutory at-risk criteria, the loss can be used to offset other positive sources of income on a member's individual tax return.

It sounds like a no-brainer. What does "amount at risk" mean? For tax purposes, it means the true amount of economic loss that one can suffer when a business activity goes sour. Realistically, one cannot lose more than the sum total of what he has invested in the business. Statutorily, said amount is defined by Section 465(b): ***Amounts Considered at Risk***. The term "amounts" (plural) means the sum of three separate at-risk items.

We paraphrase Section 465(b) as follows:

A taxpayer shall be considered at risk for an activity with respect to amounts that include—

1. the amount of money contributed to the activity,

2. the adjusted basis of other property contributed to the activity, and

*3. amounts borrowed for use in the activity to the extent that the taxpayer is **personally liable for its repayment**.* [Emphasis added.]

The requirement that a taxpayer be personally liable for the repayment of borrowed money strikes at the heart of the LLC concept. The LLC psyche, with its tunnel focus on "LL" (limited liability), makes LLCs particularly vulnerable to those financing arrangements where direct personal liability is nil. Such nil liability is the direct consequence of using unsecured promissory notes, overencumbered property, stop-loss guarantees, "part of the action," if the business succeeds, and other intangible and unenforceable security arrangements. Brilliance, sophistication, and deception are the hallmarks for using other people's money rather than one's own. The IRS calls these arrangements: *nonrecourse financing.* We call them: "finessing of financing." Since these arrangements limit each member's loss pass-throughs, why endorse them at the entity level?

Part II of Schedule K-1

Schedule K-1: **Member's Share of Income, Deductions, Credits, etc.**, consists of three parts on its front page. As edited for LLCs, these parts are captioned:

Part I — Information about the LLC **Entity**,

Part II — Information about the LLC **Member**,

Part III— Member's Share of Current Year Items.

Items L, M. and N described above constitute the focal role of ownership interests in the LLC. It is for this reason that we present a near replica of Part II in Figure 12.2. When reviewing Figure 12.2, do keep in mind that it is a *per member* statement. The checkbox, percentage, and dollar amount entries will differ, usually, for each member.

Because Part II is a per member statement, it needs to be prepared carefully and as correctly as is humanly possible. This is the task of the TMM who must examine all books, records, and contractual-type agreements and extract that which is pertinent to each member. Should questions about correctness arise, they should be referred to the Rules Committee for resolution. In any well-run business, the interpretation of questionable issues should not rest on one person alone. A Rules Committee — consisting of three to five members — would be responsible for posting and issuing a K-1 to each person or entity who was an LLC member at any time during the tax year.

Part I (Information about the LLC) will not vary from member to member. Hence, the focus of the TMM's one-time entries would be on—

Part II	Schedule K-1 (Form 1065)	Year
	INFORMATION ABOUT THE MEMBER	

G. Your Tax I.D. (SSN or EIN) ▶ _____

H. Your name, address, & ZIP _____

I. ☐ Member-manager   ☐ Other member

J. ☐ Domestic member   ☐ Foreign member

K. If entity, what type? ▶ _____

L. *Member's share of profit, loss, & capital:*

Beginning	Ending
Profit _____ %	_____ %
Loss _____ %	_____ %
Capital _____ %	_____ %

M. *Member's share of liabilities at year end:*

Nonrecourse .... $ _____

Qualified nonrecourse .... $ _____

Recourse .... $ _____

N. *Member's capital account analysis:*

Beginning capital .... $ _____

Capital contributions................. $ _____

Allocable increases/decreases ...... $ _____

Withdrawals & distributions .... $ _____

Ending capital account .... $ _____

- -

☐ Tax basis   ☐ Sec. 704(b) book

☐ GAAT   ☐ Other (explain)

Fig. 12.2 - A Member's Profit, Loss, & Capital Sharing "Analysis"

A. The LLC's Tax ID (EIN)

B. The LLC's registered name and home address, and

C. The IRS Center where Form 1065 (with all Schedules K-1 attached) is to be filed.

Hopefully, the LLC is not a publicly traded entity, nor is it a registered tax shelter. If so, entity activities and membership flexibilities are severely restrained.

Part III of Schedule K-1

There are some 20 distributive sharing (pass-through) items on Part III. For information digesting purposes, we present their edited captions in Figure 12.3. Following certain items on the official K-1, there are blank spaces. These blank spaces are for including additional information or instructions, as needed.

Part III	Schedule K-1 (Form 1065)	Year
DISTRIBUTIVELY SHARED ITEMS		

1. Ordinary income <loss>	11. Other income <loss>
2. Rental realty income <loss>	12. Sec. 179 deduction
3. Other rental income <loss>	13. Other deductions
4. Guaranteed payments	14. Self-employment earnings
5. Interest income	15. Credits & credit recapture
6. Dividend income	16. Foreign transactions
7. Royalties	17. Alternative minimum tax (AMT) items
8. Net Short-term capital gain <loss>	
	18. Tax-exempt income
9. Net long-term capital gain <loss>	19. Distributions
	20. Other information
10. Net Sec. 1231 gain <loss>	
Other as coded on page 2	*Other as coded on page 2*

Fig. 12.3 - Member's Prorata Share of Current Year Items

For example, at space 20 the caption is: *Other information.* All LLC members should be put on notice about the at-risk loss limitation rules explained above. As the TMM, you have a duty to do so. Example condensed wording might be:

If the sum of all loss pass-throughs above exceeds your ending capital account at item N in Part II, see IRC Sec. 465 re At-Risk Limitations.

We wouldn't expect every notified member to actually read Section 465 and its regulations. But the mere mention of such limitations on the K-1 is an alertness reminder. Each member will be reminded again of this at-risk feature when a loss pass-through is entered on Schedule E of Form 1040. There, a headnote to *Income or Loss from LLCs* states—

If you report a loss from an at-risk activity for which ***any*** *amount is* ***not*** *at risk, you* ***must*** *. . . attach* ***Form 6198*** [At-Risk Limitations].

In proceeding down the sharing items listed in Figure 12.3, we suggest you do so in four distinct analytical steps. After each step, you verify, crosscheck, and balance the entry amounts for all members at one time. The cross-totals must exact-match the corresponding single total amount on Schedule K: *Members'* (plural) ***Distributive Share Items***.

The four distinct steps would be—

Step 1 — Ordinary income or loss for the core business (on page 1 of Form 1065)
- apply each member's ending profit or loss percentage at item L (in Part II).

Step 2 — Rental income or loss from real estate and other rental activities (on page 3 of Form 1065: Schedule K; items 2 and 3c)
- apply the same percentages as in step 1.

Step 3 — Portfolio income or loss from investment activities
- interest, dividends, capital gains, capital losses (items 5, 6a, 8, 9a, and 10 on Schedule K).
- apply each member's capital percentage at item L (in Part II).

Step 4 — All other "tax significant" pass-through items

- guaranteed payments, Section 1231 gain or loss, Section 179 deduction, self-employment earnings, AMT items, and others (perhaps) in Figure 12.3.

Note in Step 4 that we signify tax significant items only. If a pass-through item is $10 or less, it is truly insignificant in the taxation scheme of things. In our view, the pass-through of items totaling less than $100 is also insignificant, called: *de minimis.* Compare this amount with the likely $10,000 to $100,000 or more at risk by an LLC member. As such, the $100 represents a one-thousandth percent minutia item.

At some point in the K-1 postings proves, you (as the TMM) have to draw the line against driving yourself crazy with pass-through minutiae. If you are up to the challenge, you may want to endure the minutiae just long enough to drive the IRS crazy. Technically, every 10 cent, 9 dollar, or $336.21 item on each and every Schedule K-1 is cross-matched by the IRS's computer when each member files his own income tax return. If there were 10 such items on 100 LLC member returns, that would be 1,000 items of minutiae for the IRS to process. If there were so much as a 10 cent error in each said item, think of the burden on the IRS when pumping out 1,000 trivial demands for additional tax, penalties, and interest. The IRS often creates problems for itself.

Page 2 of Schedule K-1

We raise the issue of minutiae on the K-1s for good reason. The reason is found on page 2 (which is the back side) of Schedule K-1. There, there are approximately 120 (117 by actual count) descriptive codings for the dollar amounts entered on page 1. The coding symbols are capitalized letters: A through W. The instructions at the top of page 2 say—

This list identifies the codes used on Schedule K-1 for all members and provides summarized reporting information for members who file Form 1040.

For example, at item 1: ***Ordinary business income <loss>***, it says to the K-1 recipient—

You must first determine whether the income <loss> is passive or nonpassive. Then enter on your return as follows:

* *Passive loss* — *Form 8582, line 3b*
* *Passive income* — *Sch. E, line 28, col. (g)*
* *Nonpassive loss* — *Sch. E, line 28, col. (h)*
* *Nonpassive income* — *Sch. E, line 28, col. (i)*

A few other excerpts from page 2 will illustrate the alphabetized coding of selected items:

11C — *Sec. 1256 contracts & straddles* — Form 6781, line 1

13H — *Investment interest expense* — Form 4952, line 1

15N — *Credit for research activities* — Form 6745, line 42

16L — *Foreign taxes paid* — Form 1116, Part II

17E — *Oil, gas, & geothermal deductions* — Form 6251, line 25

Now, envisage a K-1 recipient whose page 1 space 17: *Alternative minimum tax (AMT) items* shows a $62.29 amount. The amount is followed by code E: Oil, gas, & geothermal deductions (17E above). What does he do? He scrambles to get Form 6251 (AMT) and runs down the list of 27 other AMT items that have to be included. When he totals them all on line 28, if married, he *subtracts* $58,000. If he had no other AMT items than the $62.29, he's put to a lot of work — and worry — for nothing. The AMT amount of tax would be $16.20 (62.29 x 26%).

Here's where the management expertise of the GMM (general manager) comes in. Once made aware of the "minutiae problem" of the K-1s, he has to put his foot down. He needs to say to himself and to his TMM (tax manager): "We cannot grab every tax star in the universe. We are not a registered tax shelter nor an investment holding company. We'll stick to our active core business and a few solid rental properties. Get rid of all else!"

"Yes, sir," the TMM says to the GMM. "Consider it done."

Get Ahead of the Crowd

The Schedule K-1 minutiae problem is not unique among LLCs. It also pervades the K-1 world of limited partnerships and S corporations. It seems that all three pass-through entities have the same fault. Invariably, they are late in filing their annual returns with the IRS and in mailing the K-1s to their distributees. The prescribed due date is April 15th though rarely is this date ever met. The minutiae, we believe, are part of the late filing problem.

Ordinarily, when filing an LLC Form 1065, there is no IRS penalty. This is because the LLC itself is not a taxable entity. It is the pass-through members who are taxed. When the K-1s are late, each K-1 recipient is also late in filing his/her/its own tax return. This is upsetting to conscientious taxpayer-members. A well managed LLC can do better than this. It can get ahead of the K-1 crowd by filing Form 1065 and its K-1s by March 15th each year.

Because most K-1 pass-through recipients are individuals, the entity accounting year ends on December 31st. The corresponding entity filing date — and that of the K-1 recipients — is traditionally April 15th. If this date is missed, the entity can request an extension for four months, and each individual can get an automatic six-month extension. One tax extension leads to another extension, which leads to sloppy habits and late returns every year. Late filings tend to produce more errors. Memory failures, disorganized records, and hurried entries on a tax form are natural "error producers." Except for bona fide emergencies, the filing of delinquent returns is inexcusable.

As stated previously, an LLC is an internally-controlled flexible economic unit. As part of this flexibility feature, why not target Form 1065 and its Schedules K-1 to be . . . **in the mail** . . . **each year . . . on or before** March 15th?

Yes, this can be done. It requires discipline, focus, and incentive. The incentive is that you can boast proudly of being the rare LLC that is ahead of the crowd and well on your way to staying ahead.

ABOUT

THE AUTHOR

Holmes F. Crouch

Born on a small farm in southern Maryland, Holmes was graduated from the U.S. Coast Guard Academy with a Bachelor's Degree in Marine Engineering. While serving on active duty, he wrote many technical articles on maritime matters. After attaining the rank of Lieutenant Commander, he resigned to pursue a career as a nuclear engineer.

Continuing his education, he earned a Master's Degree in Nuclear Engineering from the University of California. He also authored two books on nuclear propulsion. As a result of the tax write-offs associated with writing these books, the IRS audited his returns. The IRS's handling of the audit procedure so annoyed Holmes that he undertook to become as knowledgeable as possible regarding tax procedures. He became a licensed private Tax Practitioner by passing an examination administered by the IRS. Having attained this credential, he started his own tax preparation and counseling business in 1972.

In the early years of his tax practice, he was a regular talk-show guest on San Francisco's KGO Radio responding to hundreds of phone-in tax questions from listeners. He was a much sought-after guest speaker at many business seminars and taxpayer meetings. He also provided counseling on special tax problems, such as divorce matters, property exchanges, timber harvesting, mining ventures, animal breeding, independent contractors, selling businesses, and offices-at-home. Over the past 25 years, he has prepared well over 10,000 tax returns for individuals, estates, trusts, and small businesses (in partnership and corporate form).

During the tax season of January through April, he prepares returns in a unique manner. During a single meeting, he completes the return . . . *on the spot!* The client leaves with his return signed, sealed, and in a stamped envelope. His unique approach to preparing returns and his personal interest in his clients' tax affairs have honed his professional proficiency. His expertise extends through itemized deductions, computer-matching of income sources, capital gains and losses, business expenses and cost of goods, residential rental expenses, limited and general partnership activities, closely-held corporations, to family farms and ranches.

He remembers spending 12 straight hours completing a doctor's complex return. The next year, the doctor, having moved away, utilized a large accounting firm to prepare his return. Their accountant was so impressed by the manner in which the prior return was prepared that he recommended the doctor travel the 500 miles each year to have Holmes continue doing it.

He recalls preparing a return for an unemployed welder, for which he charged no fee. Two years later the welder came back and had his return prepared. He paid the regular fee . . . and then added a $300 tip.

During the off season, he represents clients at IRS audits and appeals. In one case a shoe salesman's audit was scheduled to last three hours. However, after examining Holmes' documentation it was concluded in 15 minutes with "no change" to his return. In another instance he went to an audit of a custom jeweler that the IRS dragged out for more than six hours. But, supported by Holmes' documentation, the client's return was accepted by the IRS with "no change."

Then there was the audit of a language translator that lasted two full days. The auditor scrutinized more than $1.25 million in gross receipts, all direct costs, and operating expenses. Even though all expensed items were documented and verified, the auditor decided that more than $23,000 of expenses ought to be listed as capital items for depreciation instead. If this had been enforced it would have resulted in a significant additional amount of tax. Holmes strongly disagreed and after many hours of explanation got the amount reduced by more than 60% on behalf of his client.

He has dealt extensively with gift, death and trust tax returns. These preparations have involved him in the tax aspects of wills, estate planning, trustee duties, probate, marital and charitable bequests, gift and death exemptions, and property titling.

Although not an attorney, he prepares Petitions to the U.S. Tax Court for clients. He details the IRS errors and taxpayer facts by citing pertinent sections of tax law and regulations. In a recent case involving an attorney's ex-spouse, the IRS asserted a tax deficiency of $155,000. On behalf of his client, he petitioned the Tax Court and within six months the IRS conceded the case.

Over the years, Holmes has observed that the IRS is not the industrious, impartial, and competent federal agency that its official public imaging would have us believe.

He found that, at times, under the slightest pretext, the IRS has interpreted against a taxpayer in order to assess maximum penalties, and may even delay pending matters so as to increase interest due on additional taxes. He has confronted the IRS in his own behalf on five separate occasions, going before the U.S. Claims Court, U.S. District Court, and U.S. Tax Court. These were court actions that tested specific sections of the Internal Revenue Code which he found ambiguous, inequitable, and abusively interpreted by the IRS.

Disturbed by the conduct of the IRS and by the general lack of tax knowledge by most individuals, he began an innovative series of taxpayer-oriented Federal tax guides. To fulfill this need, he undertook the writing of a series of guidebooks that provide in-depth knowledge on one tax subject at a time. He focuses on subjects that plague taxpayers all throughout the year. Hence, his formulation of the "Allyear" Tax Guide series.

The author is indebted to his wife, Irma Jean, and daughter, Barbara MacRae, for the word processing and computer graphics that turn his experiences into the reality of these publications. Holmes welcomes comments, questions, and suggestions from his readers. He can be contacted in California at (408) 867-2628, or by writing to the publisher's address.

ALLYEAR Tax Guides
by Holmes F. Crouch

For information about the above titles, contact
Holmes F. Crouch

Allyear Tax Guides

Phone: (408) 867-2628   Fax: (408) 867-6466

224